Notions in English

# Notions in English

A course in effective communication for upper-intermediate and more advanced students

*Leo Jones*

with drawings by Peter Kneebone

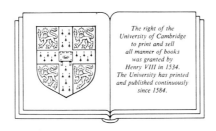

The right of the
University of Cambridge
to print and sell
all manner of books
was granted by
Henry VIII in 1534.
The University has printed
and published continuously
since 1584.

Cambridge University Press
Cambridge
London   New York   New Rochelle
Melbourne   Sydney

Published by the Press Syndicate of the University of Cambridge
The Pitt Building, Trumpington Street, Cambridge CB2 1RP
32 East 57th Street, New York, NY 10022, USA
296 Beaconsfield Parade, Middle Park, Melbourne 3206, Australia

© Cambridge University Press 1979

First published 1979
Fifth printing 1984

Printed in Great Britain by
Fletcher & Son Ltd, Norwich

ISBN 0 521 22620 1 Book
ISBN 0 521 22688 0 Cassette

# Contents

vii

## Acknowledgements

This course was developed and tested in the Anglo-Continental School of English in Bournemouth. I should like to thank the directors of the Anglo-Continental Educational Group, Mr F. Schillig and Mr G. Oetiker, for making this possible. Sincere thanks also to my friends and colleagues in the former Department of Advanced Studies, in particular Richard Denman, John Forster, Perrée Geller, Sue Gosling, Belinda Harris, Jan Milburn, Michael Roberts, and Rob Shave for all their suggestions, criticisms, encouragement and advice.

The author and publishers are grateful to the following for permission to reproduce illustrations: Reg Piggott (pages 8, 46, 82, 113 and 114): Maggie Stocking, Keystone Press Agency, Barnaby's Picture Library (page 10); Leslie Marshall (pages 16 and 17); Post Office Telecommunications (pages 19, 20 and 59); Ted Draper (pages 28, 78, 84, 130 and 150); London Transport (page 37); British Rail (page 38); the Estate of the late W. Heath Robinson and the Trustees of the British Museum (page 48); Keystone Press Agency (page 56); Rosalind Moore (page 60); Mike Cole (page 132); Matchmaker International (page 133); United Feature Syndicate Inc. (pages 151 and 152). Cover photographs by Terry Williams.

Book design by Peter Ducker

# To the student

Notions are ideas we express through language. *Notions in English* looks at general notions like 'Motion', 'Possibility' and 'Purpose' and at specific notions connected with topics like 'The weather', 'Geography' and 'Politics'. Some units in this book focus on particular general notions or particular topics. Other units concentrate more on problem areas in English, like 'Passive', 'Articles' and 'Gerunds and infinitives'.

The basic aim of *Notions in English* is to help you to communicate more effectively in English and to express yourself more accurately and confidently. Each unit has its own clearly defined aims which show exactly what you are learning and practising. These aims are listed under each unit title.

By this stage in your English learning you have received instruction in the basic grammar of English and built up a good basic vocabulary. The problem is that some areas of grammar are still 'difficult' and your spoken English may be rather inaccurate. Your active vocabulary needs to be wider. Even though you 'know' a lot, you probably have difficulty in *using* what you know. *Notions in English* will stimulate you to *use* your English and express yourself better. It will also improve your self-confidence and provide opportunities for you to correct yourself and for your teacher to correct you. But don't expect to be corrected all the time – an English lesson gives you a chance to *experiment* with English and if you are always worried about making mistakes this is impossible.

Each student in your class has built up their own personal body of knowledge of English. *Notions in English* is designed to draw on the knowledge of every member of the class. Each of you knows different things about English grammar and vocabulary. Each of you has different ideas, opinions and experiences. At this stage in your learning the traditional attitude to teachers ('My teacher knows everything – he decides what I should learn') is no longer valid. Your teacher is your language adviser – a walking dictionary possibly, but not a walking encyclopaedia ! The best person to decide what *you* need to know is *you*.

So, you must build up your own personal vocabulary and conversational techniques according to your needs and interests. In the presentation sections of each unit there will be many things you already know and use, some things you don't know, some things not presented which you know and think other students should find out about – and many things not presented which you want to know. If you want to know something you must *find it* by asking or by using a dictionary. Prepare these sections before the lesson.

In the practice activities you will be using the English you know already, as well as the language items you have recently learnt, been reminded of or found out for yourself. It is up to you to make the activities as challenging as possible. Try not to relax and 'play safe' by sticking to language you know well or by saying as little as possible. Experiment with the new language items. Be as inventive and imaginative as you can.

Remember that effective communication does not only depend on accuracy, but also on being able to express yourself confidently. *Notions in English* will help you to do this.

# To the teacher

## The language content

The basic aim of *Notions in English* is to train students to communicate effectively in English by increasing their confidence, accuracy and range of expression. Each unit focuses on different aspects of English and has particular aims which are clearly defined at the beginning of the unit. There are two types of unit:

*Topics:* These units introduce the *specific notions* students need to express in conversations in English. These range from 'The weather' to 'Politics' and apart from relevant vocabulary items, many associated conversational techniques and language functions are presented and practised.

*Problem areas:* In these units the main problem areas of English grammar are reviewed. This is done by showing how structures and vocabulary are used to express *general notions*, such as 'Motion' and 'Possibility'. Some units are more purely grammatical, such as 'Gerunds and infinitives' and 'Questions'. However, this book is not intended to be a comprehensive description of the rules of English grammar – it focuses on certain areas of English and provides practice. For a more complete description, teachers should refer to *A Communicative Grammar of English* by Geoffrey Leech and Jan Svartvik (Longman).

The terms *specific notion* and *general notion* derive from the Council of Europe's model for adult language learning: *The Threshold Level* by J. Van Ek *et al.* (Pergamon). The selection and arrangement of the language content of *Notions in English* was made on the basis of many teachers' experience of the needs and interests of adult learners from all over the world.

## Using this book

*Notion in English* is primarily a course in spoken English with some sections concentrating more on written English. It is designed to be used with *Functions of English* (New Edition CUP 1981), though it can also be used independently. If used in parallel, it is suggested that units are selected as preparation for *Functions of English* (for example *Notions in English* units 6 and 19 are useful preparation for *Functions of English* unit 4). If both books are worked through chronologically, then three units of *Notions in English* can be studied between each unit of *Functions of English*. Alternatively, there is enough variety in both courses for *Notions in English* to be completed before students move on to *Functions of English*.

*Notions in English* is not in itself a self-contained course book – students should also receive training in understanding spoken and written English, according to their needs.

Adult students at all levels from upper-intermediate to more advanced have found *Notions in English* useful and interesting. Although it is not an exam-preparation book, the contents of each unit are relevant to the needs of students preparing for an exam. It has been used successfully by many different teachers with many different types of classes.

Much of *Notions in English* may seem rather different from courses at this level you have used before. Quite simply, it is based on the needs and interests of adults from all over the world who want to improve their spoken English by *using* their English in class.

Probably the basic difference between *Notions in English* and more traditional courses is that the practice activities are more open-ended. This may leave more scope for errors (which the teacher must decide about correcting), but it leads to a creative use of the language – not just controlled manipulation.

The teacher must be alert to the needs of the class and this will involve a number of things:

a) Selection of units – the order in which the units are presented is not fixed. Some units may seem more urgent than others for a particular class. Some units may not seem essential at all. This is likely to vary from class to class.

b) Presupposed knowledge – some sections may presuppose more knowledge than a particular class possesses. Supplementary material may be required from other sources (for example *English in Situations* by Robert O'Neill (OUP)). Similarly some sections may be omitted because they are too easy for a particular class.

c) Each class has different preferences when it comes to practice. Certain practice activities may appeal to some classes and not to others. Again, you may need to select.

It will now be clear that a teacher who is either inexperienced or authoritarian will not find *Notions in English* straightforward to teach. However, any teacher who is adaptable and sensitive to his students will find the techniques used stimulating both for the class and the teacher. The learning process will be shared between the class and the teacher; lessons will be enjoyable and useful. A non-native speaker of English can certainly use *Notions in English* effectively, provided that his English is fluent and that he has an awareness of appropriateness in English.

## Presentation techniques

a) Every unit begins by listing its *aims*. It should be made clear to the students what these aims are, and that they can only be achieved by combining their previous knowledge with the new language items presented in the unit.

b) Some units contain lists of lexical items headed 'Can you use these words?' Some of these are complete lists and some require students to complete the lists themselves. These sections are designed to show students the essential lexical items for a topic and draw on their own personal vocabulary. Lists are used because this is the most economical way of presenting lexical items when each student has a different body of knowledge.

Students must find out the meaning of new words by using a dictionary *before* the lesson or by asking each other or by asking the teacher. They should be encouraged to *find out* more related words which they want to add to their own personal vocabulary. Memorizing can be helped by 'covering' the words in a list, in other words masking each column progressively from right to left until only the initial letters are visible.

c) Some units contain *useful language* directly relevant to the practice activity involved. All these expressions are useful for other situations. 3.9 is an example. These sections are recorded on the accompanying cassette.

d) Some units contain exercises which are 'tests' to find out what students know already and what they don't know. They also stimulate questions from students wishing to find out more similar language items. 3.1 and 8.7 are examples.

e) The warning note !★CAREFUL★! draws attention to problem areas – errors which are easy to make. 29.1 and 29.2 have examples.

The presentation sections vary according to the language items being revised or introduced. The revision of passive knowledge and the acquisition of new language items depend not only on the presentation material, but also on the teacher's awareness of the students' difficulties and needs and the students' own willingness to find out and ask for the language they personally need.

Many of the activities in *Notions in English* depend on students working together – in pairs, in groups or as a class. Although this means they may be speaking English freely without interruptions for correction, it does *not* mean that the teacher should fail to 'monitor' each speaker and take action if difficulties or errors are overheard. The teacher may sometimes ask groups to 'perform' in front of the rest of the class as a check on accuracy and achievement. Students should be encouraged to strike a reasonable balance between being adventurous in their experiments with English and asking for help or guidance when they need it. The point must be made that in later freer stages of practice – as in real life – making mistakes is far less serious than failing to communicate.

## Practice activities

As some of the practice activities may involve unfamiliar techniques, here are brief notes on the commonly used practice methods and their rationale.

a) *Pattern conversations* and *typical interaction:* These provide two types of pattern: a pattern of language for controlled practice which is reassuring for students using new language items for the first time *and* a 'behavioural pattern' in italics on the right. This 'behavioural pattern' shows the direction the interaction takes and can be used as a cue to help students move away from the printed text on the left. As soon as students feel more confident they can move away from the pattern sentences and introduce their own variations, later they can change the direction of the interaction, if they wish. An example of this is 3.2. The pattern conversations are all recorded on the cassette.

b) *Role-playing:* These improvisation ideas fall into two types: roles which students may actually have to play in real life (3.3 for example) and fantasy roles chosen because they give greater scope for interesting creative language production (10.3 for example). Some of these activities may require one student to use the book while his partner keeps his closed (9.6 for example). These activities work best if the roles are written out onto 'role-cards' – blank postcards are ideal – so that each student can concentrate easily on the role he is playing.

c) *Games:* These make the routine practice of language items more entertaining even though they may often be pure manipulation exercises. Examples are unit 11 and 15.3.

d) *Your own experiences and ideas:* A large number of activities involve the students in talking about themselves, their memories, their plans, hopes, opinions and so on. Examples are 7.4 and 14.4.

e) *Talking points:* These discussion topics stimulate a free exchange of opinions, using the new language items presented earlier. Groups of three or four may be found more productive to start the ball rolling, then each group reports and the ensuing discussion may involve the whole class. Students should be given a chance to select the talking points that interest them most. Examples are 27.4 and 32.3.

f) *Questionnaires:* These projects are suitable for use in an English-speaking country *or* in a non-English-speaking country. The questionnaires enable other people's ideas to enter the classroom, providing a window on the world outside. Students learning in an English-speaking country may need a thorough rehearsal before they feel competent to carry out their first questionnaire, but the extra practice outside class they will get makes this time well spent. In a non-English-speaking country students should ask fellow-countrymen the same questions (in their own language) and report the answers they have received to the class in *English*. Examples are 3.5 and 7.3.

g) *Simulations:* These give scope for extended free production over a whole lesson or even longer. Students are given roles to play and tasks to carry out and require very little prompting once the activity is under way. A wide range of language skills is used, as well as the new language items. Examples are 7.6 and 25.5.

h) *Write:* These short written assignments allow students to consolidate what they have learnt and communicate in writing. Examples are 27.5 and 47.2. Further relevant writing practice, particularly in the form of reports or letters, will suggest itself at many other stages in each unit.

i) *Exercises:* The format of the exercises in units 48, 49, 50 and part of unit 31 is specially devised to enable students to learn and revise the language items at home. As explained in unit 49, only a small part of the work should be done during valuable class time. Units 48–50 should be 'dipped into' at regular intervals – not left to be done all together at the end of the course. The decision when to do them and how often will depend on the length and intensity of a particular course.

Not all practice activities can be categorized as briefly as those above. The language being practised may require more unusual activities, like 37.5. Such activities – like all the practice activities in *Notions in English* – are intended to be both enjoyable *and* relevant to the needs of the students.

## The recording

Sections of the text which are recorded on the cassette accompanying this book are indicated by the symbol: [cassette symbol]

The recording has two principal uses: to focus attention on aspects of stress, intonation and tone of voice (especially in *pattern conversation* and *useful language* sections) and as an aural key to some practice sections. It is also a useful way of introducing some sections. It will be found that it is much more convenient to discuss or analyse features like stress, intonation and tone of voice by using the cassette than by the teacher reading aloud. The teacher will need to stop the cassette when he wishes students to repeat what they have heard.

## The Key

Exercises and presentation sections marked with the symbol: [key symbol] have solutions in the Key at the back of the book. Note that the lists of lexical items in the Key are to be considered as a minimum amount of essential lexis – students should be encouraged to suggest or ask for additional lexis. (Note also that the solutions to 2.2 *are* in the key.)

## Picture cards

One of the disadvantages of the enclosed world of the classroom is that the real world seems remote. This can be counteracted by bringing the outside world into class, using home-made *picture cards*. These are easy and fun to make by collecting large magazine pictures and mounting them on stiff card. Frequently used picture cards may need protecting with non-reflective adhesive film.

Picture cards can be built up into sets to illustrate each topic covered in *Notions in English*. For example: Transport – pictures of cars, trains and planes; Home – pictures of houses, furniture; Food – pictures of fruit, vegetables and utensils; Holidays – pictures of holiday resorts and pages of brochures; and so on with other topics.

## Supplementary texts and exercises

Teachers using *Notions in English* might consider supplementing the practice in the book with material from other sources. In particular: topical reading texts from newspapers and magazines, recorded listening extracts from radio programmes and home-made live recordings, even relevant slot-filler exercises from more 'traditional' books. These should be chosen to suit the specific needs and interest of a class in the personal way that no course-book can attempt. Such texts and exercises could link up with each of the topics and grammatical notions dealt with in *Notions in English*, thus providing extra practice and consolidation.

## Supplementary role-playing material

The series *Q-Cards* by Saxon Menné (Paul Norbury) is specially recommended for further role-playing practice of the following units of *Notions in English*:

Unit 14 Money      Q-Cards 'The budget meeting'
Unit 27 Education  Q-Cards 'The parent–teacher meeting'
Unit 34 Work       Q-Cards 'Interview for a job'
Unit 42 Crime      Q-Cards 'The detective'
Unit 46 Sport      Q-Cards 'Press conference'

Similarly, with a large class, the pack *It's Your Choice* by Michael Lynch (Edward Arnold), provides extra role-playing practice of these *Notions in English* units:

Unit  7 Entertainment 'Pop festival'
Unit  9 Transport     'Motorway'
Unit 12 Home          'The future of Glosthorpe'
Unit 23 Geography     'Oil threat to Radleigh'
Unit 27 Education     'Smith Street Comprehensive'
Unit 42 Crime         'Violence in Blanting'

## For reference

The following books are useful and relevant to students and teachers using *Notions in English*:
*A Communicative Grammar of English* by Geoffrey Leech and Jan Svartvik (Longman)
*Longman Dictionary of Contemporary English* (Longman)

# 1 The weather

Describing the weather
Describing the climate of a region or country
Commenting on the weather to start a conversation
Reporting the weather forecast

 **1.1 What's the weather like?**

The sun's shining.

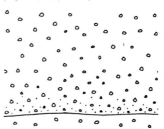

It looks like rain.

It's pouring with rain.

It's snowing quite heavily.

What other comments could you make on each picture?

## 1.2 Can you use these words?

Ask someone to explain the ones you aren't sure about.

| | | | |
|---|---|---|---|
| mild | freezing | thunderstorm | drizzle |
| clear | cool | hurricane | hail |
| close | misty | monsoon | mist |
| chilly | foggy | gale | fog |
| windy | hazy | blizzard | haze |
| boiling | damp | frost | drought |
| | | | flood |

A: It's ... for the time of year, isn't it?
B: Yes, quite a contrast to yesterday's ...

In pairs, make up more conversations following the pattern. When you feel confident enough, leave the pattern and start to improvise! Continue your conversations beyond the opening lines.

7

## 1.3   The climate in different seasons

A:  What's the climate like in Bournemouth?
B:  It's quite mild during the winter, the spring's often windy and it rains a lot, the summer's fairly warm and sunny, and in the autumn it starts to get cool and it's sometimes foggy.

Ask and answer similar questions about the other places on the map. Also ask: 'Would you like to live there?' and 'Why?' or 'Why not?'

Describe in more detail the climate for each month of your own region or country, and other countries you have visited.


## 1.4   Lovely day, isn't it?

What's wrong with this?    A:  Lovely day, isn't it?
                           B:  Yes, the sun is shining.

In a typical interaction, A comments on the weather and shows his feelings. B responds by echoing the feeling or being optimistic or pessimistic. Like this:

A:  Lovely day, isn't it?
B:  Mm, marvellous!                *Echo*
or  Yes, it makes a nice change!   *Optimistic*
or  Well, let's hope it lasts!     *Pessimistic*

Think of three similar replies to these comments:

'Awful, this rain, isn't it?'
'This wind's very annoying, isn't it?'
'Very chilly for the time of year, isn't it?'

'This sunshine's fantastic, isn't it?'
'What dreadful weather!'
'Turned out nice again, hasn't it?'
'I don't like the look of those clouds, do you?'

Act out conversations in pairs from these pictures:

## 1.5 Weather forecasts

Here is the outlook for tomorrow:

| 10°C | heavy rain | gale force winds |

'The forecast says it'll be quite cool and it's going to rain heavily. And it's going to be extremely windy. So it sounds like a day to stay at home and do some reading.'

Here are some more forecasts. Report them in the same way and discuss how the weather will affect your activities:

| 20°C | cloudy | no wind |
| —10°C | clear sky | windy |
| 30°C | hazy | no wind |
| 0°C | snow | strong winds |
| 5°C | fog | no wind |
| 15°C | showers | windy |

Look at the 'Weather Around The World' in a newspaper. What's the weather like in different cities and how would it affect your activities there?

Look at tomorrow's *real* weather forecast and talk about it. Was the forecast they gave for today accurate?

## 1.6 Write

Write a description of the weather this morning when you left home, the same time yesterday, the same time a week ago and during your last holiday.

# 2   Questions

Asking Yes/No and Wh– questions accurately

## 2.1   Yes/No questions

| | |
|---|---|
| Is ...? | Was ...? |
| Are ...? | Were ...? |
| Does ...? | Did ...? |
| Do ...? | |
| Has ...? | Had ... before? |
| Have ...? | Had ... previously? |
| Can ...? | |
| Will ...? | Could ...? |
| | Would ...? |

Ask one question of each type about each of these photos:

## 2.2 'Mysteries'

Solve the following mysteries by asking your teacher questions. Each question must be perfectly accurate, otherwise you won't get an answer. Only 'Yes' or 'No' answers will be given.

1 A woman went into a bar and asked for a glass of water. The barman pointed a gun at her. She thanked him and went out.
2 A man was found lying dead in the middle of a desert. He had a pack on his back.
3 A woman dialled a number on the telephone. Someone answered and said 'Hallo !' She put the phone down with a happy smile.
4 A man is found dead in a room. There is no furniture and all the doors and windows are locked from the inside. There is a pool of water on the floor.
5 There's a man on a bed and a piece of wood on the floor. A second man comes into the room with sawdust on his hands, smiles and goes out again.

## 2.3 Wh– questions

| | | |
|---|---|---|
| Who ...? | What ...? | How ...? |
| Who ... to? | What sort of ...? | How many ...? |
| Who ... from? | What ... like? | How much ...? |
| Whose ...? | What ...? | How often ...? |
| | | How long ...? |
| Which ...? | Why ...? | |
| | Where ...? | |
| | When ...? | |

Ask one question of each type about each of these cartoons:

Ask one question of each type using magazines or picture cards. Do this in pairs – one holds the picture and answers the other's questions.

### 2.4 Game: 'Who am I?'

Each player thinks of a famous historical or fictional character. Everyone else has to find out who he is, but they are only allowed to ask *one* of each type of question. 'Who are you?' is not permitted.

### 2.5 'Press conference'

Four people have just arrived in town: an explorer, an inventor, an astronaut and a round-the-world sailor. Interview each one.

### 2.6 Game: 'Alibis'

Two people go out of the room for a few minutes to work out what they were doing together at 3 p.m. yesterday when a robbery took place.
Each one is interrogated separately by everyone else. Each difference in their stories means one year in prison.

Then two different people are sent out to do the same. Choose a different time and crime for each round.

## 3 Shops

Shopping in different shops and stores
Describing shopping experiences
Describing shopping habits
Paying compliments and responding to them

### 3.1 Shops

Where would you buy the things on this shopping list?

# Shopping List

soap
hammer
oranges
fish
envelopes
cigarettes
flowers

magazine
butter
cassette recorder
chair
tennis racket
stamps
bracelet.

### 3.2 In a shop: typical interaction

| | | |
|---|---|---|
| Assistant: | Can I help you? | *Offer* |
| Customer: | No, it's alright thanks, I'm just looking. | *Rejection* |
| | No thanks, I'd just like to have a look around. | |
| *or* | Yes please, I'd like some … | *Vague request* |
| | Yes please, have you got any …? | |
| Assistant: | Certainly, how many …? | |
| | Certainly, how much would you like? | |
| Customer: | A large/small/medium-size jar/packet/pack/carton/can/tin/box/bottle/bag please. | *Specific request* |

You want to buy the things on this list. Act out the scene, specifying the quantity of each item you want.

# Shopping List

Coffee      baked beans      toffees
tea      lager      honey
playing cards      washing powder
paper clips      matches      typing paper
sherry      glue      chocolates

### 3.3 'The party'

*In pairs*    Half the students play the roles of customers, the other half the roles of shopkeepers. The shopkeepers stay put, but the customers have to move from one 'shop' to the next.

*Customers:*   You are having a fancy-dress party and you want to buy: funny hats, balloons, streamers, paper cups and those things you blow which make a funny noise and have a feather on the end.
You'll need to try several shops before you get everything.

    **Useful language**

I wonder if you stock …
I'm looking for …
Do you happen to know where I could find …?

*Shopkeepers:* You only stock *one* of the items you are asked for.

    **Useful language**

Well, we've got some … I can show you.
You could try the shop next door.

### 3.4 'Clothes'

Reverse the roles you played in 3.3.

*Customers:* You want to buy:
       a navy-blue Shetland pullover
       a pair of brown leather walking boots
       a pair of red knitted woollen gloves
       a tartan woollen scarf
       a waterproof red nylon anorak

Unfortunately, each shop you try can't offer you *exactly* what you want – the colour, material or size are wrong. Try all the shops in the area.

 **Useful language**

That's not quite what I'm looking for.
Is this the only sort you have?
I think I'll leave it, thanks just the same.

*Shopkeepers:* You can't supply *exactly* what each customer wants but try to persuade him to buy something in your shop.

## 3.5 Questionnaire: ask five people

This is the first of several questionnaires in this course. The idea is for you to find out information and opinions from English-speaking people outside the classroom. (If you are studying in a non-English-speaking country you should ask other people of your own nationality and then later you report their answers *in English* to the class.) Make notes of the replies you get or use a cassette recorder.

Rehearse this opening speech in class first:

'Excuse me, I wonder if you have a moment to spare. I'm a student from … and\* our class has been asked to do a sort of public opinion poll. Would you mind if I asked you a few questions – it won't take long!'
(\*Leave out the first part of the speech when talking to someone you know well.)

You may prefer to do this first questionnaire with some moral support from a class-mate! Or even to rehearse the whole interaction before trying it in real life.

> QUESTIONNAIRE ON SHOPPING
>
> 1. Where do you do your food shopping?
>    May I ask why you shop there?
>
> 2. Have food prices risen a lot recently?
>    Why is this so?
>
> 3. Where do you do your shopping for clothes?
>
> 4. What has been your biggest purchase recently?
>
> 5. If times were harder, what expenses would you try to cut?
>
> Thank you very much indeed for your time.

## 3.6 Results of the questionnaire

Exchange experiences of actually doing the questioning. Was it as bad as you expected?

Report the answers to the questions and the conclusions you have drawn.

What are your own answers to the questions?

15

### 3.7  Can you use these words?

| | | |
|---|---|---|
| chain store | cash desk | discount |
| department store | counter | service |
| market stall | show-room | delivery charge |
| corner shop | shop window | pay by cheque |

### 3.8  Talking points

*In groups*  1  Describe the shops in your country. How are they different from British shops?
2  How are the shopping habits of people in your country different?
3  Tell each other about an experience you have had shopping in Britain.

Report your discussion to the other groups.

### 3.9  Compliments

A: That's a very nice cardigan, is it new?
B: Yes, I've just bought it. I'm glad you like it.
*or* Yes, it was very cheap. I got it in a sale.
A: I like it very much. It suits you very well.
B: Oh, thank you.

#### Useful language

That's a really nice …
What a nice …
I like your …
Oh, do you really think so?
Oh, it's nice of you to say so.
You've really made my day!
Oh no, it's just an old …
Oh no, I just haven't worn it much recently.
Oh no, I've had this for ages.

In pairs, compliment each other on all the clothes and accessories you're wearing.

Compliment your teacher on his or her handwriting, teaching techniques, clothes, hairstyle and accent.

## 3.10 Clothing: American English terms

Several garments have different names in the United States and Britain. Can you 'translate' these American terms into British English:

| USA | GB |
|---|---|
| suspenders | braces |
| vest | |
| pants | |
| necktie | |
| shorts | |
| panti-hose | |
| sneakers | |
| tuxedo | |

You may not need to *use* all these American terms, but you probably *will* need to understand them. Note that although British people often understand Americanisms, the Americans don't often understand Britishisms!

Cover up the right-hand column and test yourself (or your neighbour).

# 4 The telephone

Using the telephone
Describing your experiences of and feelings about telephoning

## 4.1 Essential language

Can you use these words?

| | |
|---|---|
| directory *or* phone book | ring up |
| ex-directory | slot |
| operator | dial |
| exchange | receiver |
| telephonist | coin-box |
| engaged | |

### Useful phrases

This is … speaking.
Can I speak to …?
Could I leave a message for …?
Would you ask … to call me back, please?
I'd like to make an ADC call to …   (= 'Advice of duration and charge')
I'd like to make a transferred charge call to …
I'd like to make a personal call to …
It's cheaper after 6 and at weekends.
I'll put you through to …
I'm sorry, I didn't recognize your voice over the phone.

In pairs, practise using the essential language like this:

A: Making the call.
B: Receiving the call.

## 4.2 Telephone situations

*In pairs
back to back*

One of you is:

a) Phoning a theatre in London to inquire about the play *Romeo and Juliet*. Ask for all the relevant information including: times and dates of performance, availability of tickets, how to book and pay.

b) Phoning the police to get them to come to the scene of a motoring accident. No-one has been hurt but your car has been damaged and it wasn't your fault. The police want to know the important details before they come.

c) Phoning your boss to explain why you can't come to work on Monday morning. You have missed work several times this month already.

d) Phoning a seaside hotel to book a double room for this weekend. The hotel has been recommended, but you want details of the facilities it offers.

e) Phoning Mr Day to inquire about this job. Find out about salary, hours and conditions of work, duties. Tell him about your experience and qualifications.

> **TRAINEE** sales person to work in new exciting service business must be of smart appearance and well spoken. Income well above average. For appointment, ring Mr. Day, Bournemouth 83993, evenings 073253.

f) Phoning a garage to find out about this car you like the sound of. Check on the information given and arrange a test drive. The price seems £200 too high.

> **TRIUMPH** 2·5 P1 saloon, 1974. One private owner, genuine mileage of 23,000 approx. since new. Auto trans., power assisted steering, radio, cloth upholstery, heated rear window, reclining seats. Ice blue with darker blue inside                £1,895

## 4.3 Are you a 'telephone person'?

*In groups*  Answer 'Yes', 'No' or 'Sometimes' to these questions:

Do you prefer to write rather than phone?
When the phone rings, do you hope someone else will answer it for you?
Do you put off making phone calls till the last moment?
Do you keep your calls as short as possible?
If a phone is ringing does it *have to* be answered?

Discuss your answers to the questions. To what extent are you a 'telephone person'? (Mostly 'Yes' answers mean you aren't, mostly 'No' answers mean you are.)

## 4.4 What can go wrong?

*In groups*  Things sometimes go wrong when you try to make a phone call. Add to this list of possible things that can go wrong and what you would say and do:

| *What can go wrong?* | *What would you say and do?* |
|---|---|
| Telephone rings but no reply. | I'll try again later. |
| | *or* He's probably gone out. |
| | *or* There's no answer. |

A stranger answers.
You hear a repeated single note.
You hear rapid pips.

## 4.5 How to use a public phone

Explain to the others how to make a call from a public phone (call box or payphone) in Britain. And in your own country.

### 4.6 Telephone facilities

If you can, ring up these services. You can find the numbers in the phone book:

Dial-a-Disc
Motoring
Recipe
Time
Weather Forecast
Teletourist
(They are all recorded, so you needn't say anything yourself.)

Report to the others what you have found out. Do you have any similar services in your country?

### 4.7 Videophones: write or discuss

Combined telephones and televisions have already been developed and tested. Would you like to use one or have one in your home? Why (not)?

### 4.8 'Call me!': American English

There are a number of American terms that are not used in Britain. Can you find the British equivalent of these words and phrases:

| *USA* | *GB* |
|---|---|
| Call me! | Phone me! |
| an unlisted number | |
| Central | |
| to make a collect call person to person | |
| station to station | |
| Are you through? | |

© Post Office Telecommunications 1976

# 5 Drinks

Ordering and offering different drinks
Talking about drinking habits

## 5.1 In a bar

 Useful language

| | |
|---|---|
| What would you like? | *Offering* |
| Can I get you a drink? | |
| Same again? | |
| It's my round. | |
| I'll get these. | |

I'd like …          *Requesting*
Could I have …?

I'd better not – I'm driving.   *Refusing*
No thanks, I'm fine.

*Beer:* draught bitter
     a pint of …
     a half of …
     shandy
*Spirits:* Scotch | with ice
                | with soda
                | on its own
     Gin and tonic
*Aperitifs:* … with ice and lemon
*Wine:* dry, sweet, medium, rosé, sparkling
*Soft drinks:* bitter lemon, fruit juice

Add more drinks to the categories above.

Imagine you are in a bar. Act out the situation, using the expressions suggested.

When you are in a bar, what do you normally have? Is it customary to buy rounds in your country, as it is in Britain?

Describe your favourite drinks. Why do you like them?

### 5.2  Talking point: licensing hours in Britain

In most English towns the pubs are open at these times:

Weekdays: 11.00 a.m. – 2.30 or 3.00 p.m.
6.00 p.m. – 10.30 or 11.00 p.m.
Sundays: 12.00 noon – 2.00 p.m.
7.00 p.m. – 10.30 p.m.

Ask some English people why. Do they mind? Do you mind?


### 5.3  Talking points

*In groups*  How are bars and cafés different in your country from British ones?
What are the laws on drinking and driving?
If there is prohibition (alcohol is forbidden), why?
How is the beer in your country different from British beer?

### 5.4  Talking point: drunkenness

Can you use these words and expressions?

tee-totaller
occasional drinker
social drinker
heavy drinker
drunk
alcoholic

What do you do if you are with someone who is very drunk? How do you feel?
Is alcoholism a social problem in your country?

# 6 The past

Using past tense and perfective aspect accurately and appropriately

## 6.1 Past experiences

A: Do you *read* many *novels*?                                        *Many?*
B: Yes, I suppose I've *read* about *four novels* …                    *Number*
*or* No, I've only *read two novels* | this year.
                                     | this week.
                                     | since January.
                                     | during the last month.
A: I see, and what was the last *novel* you *read*?                     *Last one?*
B: Let me see, it was …                                                *Title*
A: And when did you *read* it?                                         *When?*
B: I *read* it | on Tuesday evening.                                   *Time*
              | in April.
              | three weeks ago.
              | the day before yesterday.
A: Why did you *read* it?                                              *Tell me more*
   Tell me about it.
   What exactly …
B: Well, …                                                            *Details*

In pairs, follow the same pattern, starting off from these prompts:

| magazines | meals     | lessons  |
|-----------|-----------|----------|
| films     | surprises | lectures |
| plays     | shocks    | jobs     |
| journeys  | cars      | letters  |
|           |           | holidays |

! *CAREFUL* ! about irregular verb forms.

## 6.2 Holidays and visits

*In small groups*  Try to find out as much information as you can from the others in your group about the
countries they have been to.
Begin by asking:       'Have you ever been to …?'
Continue by asking:  'When …?'
                     'How long …?'
                     'Where exactly …?'
                     'Who … with?'

'What exactly did you do there?'
'What sort of time did you have there?'
'Where else have you been?'

If there is time, talk about the places you have been to in Britain (or in your own country).

### 6.3 Present activities: How long? and How many? or How much?

A: Do you smoke?
B: Yes I do.
A: *How long* have you been smoking for?
B: Six years.
*or* Since 1973.
A: And *how many* cigarettes have you smoked during that time?
B: Thousands.

In pairs, ask each other about these activities. Follow the same pattern:
driving
learning English
working or studying
playing football
gambling

Report what you have found out about your partner to the other groups.

!\*CAREFUL\*! about 'for' and 'since'.

### 6.4 Changing activities: 'Bad habits'

He used to smoke and drink too much. But not any more.
He smoked and drank too much until he got married.
He hasn't smoked or drunk at all since he got married.

Since his marriage, Joe has become a new man. Here are more of his former bad habits. Use the same patterns to describe the changes:

24

late nights
scruffy clothes
laziness
inconsiderateness
greediness
lack of exercise
wasting money
getting drunk
being rude to people

### 6.5 'New year resolutions'

*In small groups*   Imagine it is December 31st last year. Think of all the new leaves you want to turn over. Make a list.

Now time has passed and we are back to today. Tell each other what resolutions you have kept or not. Begin like this:

'I'm very proud of myself because | I've ...'
                                       | I haven't ...'

*or* 'I'm ashamed to say | I've ...'
                       | I haven't ...'

### 6.6 Big events in your life

*In groups*   Talk about some of the big events that have happened to you and the decisions you have made in your life. Discuss how your life has changed – go into as much detail as you can. Talk about things like leaving school, going away from home, travelling to a foreign country and so on. Report back to everyone else when you are ready.

### 6.7 Recent activities

*In pairs*   Ask each other questions following this pattern:

A: What were you doing at ... o'clock on ... day?
B: I was ...
A: What else did you do that day?
B: I ...

Times: 7   8   9   10   11   12   1   2   3   4   5   6   7   8   9   10   11   12
Days: Monday   Tuesday   Wednesday   Thursday   Friday   Saturday   Sunday

!*CAREFUL*! about irregular verbs.

Re-enact the same situation. Imagine you are a detective questioning a suspect. The suspect is also a detective and he suspects the other one!

## 6.8 Simultaneous activities

Look at these sentences:

| While | he was playing the piano, his |
| All the time | teacher was sitting behind him. |
| At the same time as | |

During his piano lesson his teacher was sitting
behind him.

He was playing the piano.

| All the time | his teacher was sitting behind him. |
| At the same time | |

Following the same patterns, make more similar sentences about these simultaneous
activities:

John: TV  
      book  
      lesson  
      interview  
      cinema  
      football  
      disco

Mary: knitting  
      record  
      walk  
      school  
      home  
      tennis  
      bed

## 6.9 Interrupted actions

A: I was | just about to | have a swim when I saw the shark.  
        | just going to |

B: That's nothing! | I was in the middle of swimming when *I* saw the shark.  
    It was alright for you! |

A: What happened? What did you do?

B: I started swimming for the shore, of course.

26

In pairs, follow the pattern and make up similar conversations for these prompts:

bath–telephone
TV–doorbell
homework–lights went out
dinner–blackout
lift–power cut
walk–rain
beach–thunderstorm
mountain–blizzard

Think of two more similar situations.

## 6.10 Picture story

Using the language practised in this unit write or tell the story on page 28.

# 7 Entertainment

Talking about television, radio and films
Expressing your own reactions to entertainment

## 7.1 British broadcasting: in brief

BBC 1: middle-brow
BBC 2: rather more high-brow ⎱— TV Licence fees
ITV: more low-brow — advertising revenue

BBC Radio 1: pop
    2: light music and sport
    3: classical music and the arts
    4: current affairs and talk

BBC local radio stations: local interest programmes
Independent local radio: pop and local interest (advertising)
BBC World Service: programmes in English 24 hours a day

Which TV channel and which radio station do you watch or listen to most in Britain? Why?

Describe the broadcasting system in your own country. Which channel and station do you prefer?

## 7.2 Can you use these words?

programme
channel
mass media
peak viewing time

director

documentary
movie

What other people are involved in TV and radio? Add them to the list.
What other types of programme are there?

### 7.3  Questionnaire: ask five people

If this is your first questionnaire, look back to 3.5 (page 15).

> ENTERTAINMENT SURVEY
>
> 1. How many hours do you watch TV each day?
> 2. What's your favourite programme? Why?
> 3. Have you got a colour TV? Why (not)?
> 4. What annoys you most about TV?
> 5. When do you listen to the radio?
> 6. How often do you go to the cinema?
> 7. What's your favourite sort of film? Why?
>
> Thank you very much indeed for answering these questions.

Report the results of your survey.

What are your own answers to the questions?

### 7.4  Reactions to entertainment

 Useful language

I thought it was...
I was really impressed by ...
The best part was when ...
What I really liked was ...
What struck me most was ...

| The | photography | was | brilliant. |
| | script | | appalling. |
| | acting | | dreadful. |
| | | | mediocre. |
| | | | thrilling. |

Think of a bad and a good TV programme you've watched recently. And a bad and a good film. Write down the titles.

In groups, describe your reactions to the programmes and films you have noted.

In groups, compare your reactions to films or programmes *several* of you have seen.

!★DON'T USE★! the words 'boring', 'interesting', 'good' or 'bad' in this practice.

### 7.5  Talking point

*In groups*  The effect of TV on family life, conversation, radio, the cinema, the theatre. What are your experiences and views?

Report your discussion to the other groups.

### 7.6 'This evening's viewing'

*In three groups* You are TV programme controllers, planning a balanced evening's TV. Each group is aiming at a different audience: high-brow, low-brow and middle-brow.

When you have finished, introduce your channel's viewing to the 'viewers', using the board.

# 8  Numbers and letters

Saying numbers, mathematical expressions and common abbreviations
Spelling aloud

## 8.1  Saying numbers

Read these numbers aloud:

Dates:  4.9.77  24.8.63  7.7.43  (GB)
         9/4/77  8/24/63  7/7/43  (USA)

Years:  1066  1776  1801  1918  2000  55 B.C.

Telephones:  0202 27414     01 483 2911  0304 23877
             (code) (number)  01 441 4466  0473 58905

British roads:  A35  A338  M3  M27  B4120
                A12  A120  A45  M6  B3040

British cars:  P*EL*                    159*M*
               (These two letters show   (This letter shows the year of registration:
               the area of origin)       S = 1977–8   T = 1978–9   V = 1979–80)
               RPV 418R  SLJ 307T  GJJ 433S  WVR 707P

Add two more numbers to each category. Then dictate them to your neighbour.

## 8.2  Arithmetic

*In pairs*  The student on the left must cover up the left-hand column below. The one on the right must cover up the right-hand column. Now give the instructions slowly enough for your partner to do the arithmetic in his head.

| | |
|---|---|
| 144 + 3 | 4 + 7 |
| +7 | ×6 |
| −23 | +14 |
| −1 | −9 |
| ÷2 | −15 |
| −45 | ÷7 |
| ×5 | +4 |
| +1 | ×2 |
| −99 | +12 |
| +2 | ×4 |

### 8.3 Maths

 Can you say these aloud?

| | | | |
|---|---|---|---|
| 1.421 | $\frac{3}{4}$ | $\pi$ | 25% |
| 2,043 | $\frac{2}{3}$ | $\pi r^2$ | 25 sq km |
| $73^2$ | $\frac{7}{8}$ | $x^2 = 2^7$ | 33 cc |
| $\frac{7}{2}$ | $\sqrt{47}$ | 2,000,000 | |

In pairs write down more mathematical symbols and dictate them to another pair.

### 8.4 Spelling

*In pairs*   As fast as you can, spell these words aloud:

kneel        knit
knowledge    knock
knuckle      knife
knickers
knot
knack
knight
knob

comb
lamb
numb
thumb
bomb
limb
dumb
climb

reign
campaign
foreign
resign

gnaw
gnome
gnat

whistle
thistle
soften
fasten
castle
hasten
wrestle
listen

wrist
wreck
wrinkle
wriggle
wrap
wretched
Wright

walk
chalk
folk
calm
salmon
palm
behalf
yolk
almond
half

thought
though
thorough
through
bough
fight
height
neighbour
freight
bought
slight

| BUT | AND |
|---|---|
| laugh | ghost |
| cough | ghastly |
| rough | |
| draught | |
| enough | |

Cover up the lists above and test each other on the words.
Say one of the words and get your partner to spell it.

33

## 8.5   Personal details

Give the others in your class the following information about yourself.
Spell words aloud, if necessary. They should write down the details.

your full name
your address
your telephone number
your car registration number
your passport number
your date and place of birth

## 8.6   Telegrams

*In pairs*   Secretly write a telegram (any subject) to someone in your country in your own language or in English. Imagine you are telephoning an English-speaking telephone operator. Sit back-to-back with your partner and dictate the telegram to the operator.

## 8.7   Common abbreviations

What do these mean?
When are they used?
Read them aloud!

| | | | | |
|---|---|---|---|---|
| RSVP | P.T.O. | Ave. | A.D. | BBC |
| etc | Ltd | Rd | B.C. | VAT |
| c/o | & Co. | St | a.m. | TUC |
| approx. | v. | Gdns | p.m. | AA |
| p.p. | P.S. | Sq. | M.P. | RAC |
| i.e. | V.I.P. | Pk | | PC |
| e.g. | Gt | Cres. | | EEC |

Look at an English newspaper and find more abbreviations to add to the list.

# 9 Transport

Talking about cars, trains and buses
Asking about and explaining routes and timetables
Describing journeys

## 9.1 Cars

Draw a car and label the parts.

Imagine you are sitting in your car. Where are the important parts? Name them all. Begin like this:
'I'm sitting in the driving seat with my hands on the steering wheel. In front of me ...'

## 9.2 At a garage

 *In pairs*

| | |
|---|---|
| Motorist: | There seems to be something wrong with the ... |
| Receptionist: | The ...? What's the problem exactly? |
| Motorist: | Well, you see ... |
| Receptionist: | I see, well, it'll take about ... hours to put that right. |
| Motorist: | Fine. I'll come back at about ... o'clock then. |

Act out the situation in pairs following the same pattern. Mention different parts of the car which have gone wrong or been damaged. Ask your teacher for help with vocabulary if you need it.

## 9.3 Traffic signs

Can you explain what the signs here and on the next page mean? Find the briefest explanation of each as well as the clearest, for example:

*Briefest:* No right turn
*Clearest:* You can't turn right there, so you'd better go straight on and take the next right.

35

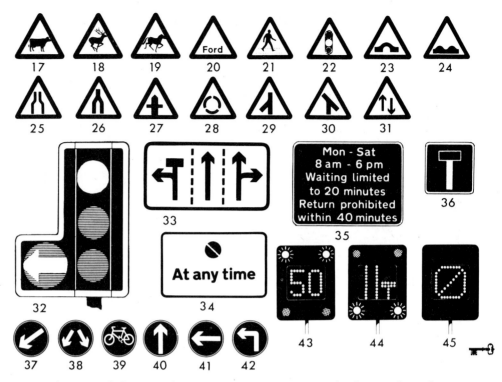

Do you have any different traffic signs in your country? Describe them or draw them.

## 9.4 Questionnaire: ask five people

(See 3.5, page 15)

TRANSPORT SURVEY

1. How do you travel to work or to the town centre? Why?
2. If you own a car, what sort is it and why did you choose it?
3. If you are in a car, do you wear a seat belt?
4. What do you think of the bus and train service here?
5. Do you walk or cycle very often?

Thank you very much for helping.

Report the results of your survey to the class.

What are your own answers to the questions?

## 9.5 Explaining routes

 At Liverpool Street Station:

Tourist:    Excuse me. I'm a bit lost, can you help me?
Londoner:   Certainly, where are you trying to get to?

| Tourist: | I'm making for *Victoria Station*. |
|---|---|
| Londoner: | *Victoria Station?* ↓ |
| Tourist: | That's right. |
| Londoner: | Well, the best way to get there is to take the *Central* line *westbound* as far as *Oxford Circus*. Then change to the *Victoria* line *southbound* and it's two stops later. Alright? |
| Tourist: | Yes, fine. Thanks very much. |
| Londoner: | Not at all. |

Act out the scene, paying attention to your intonation. Stand up.

Now follow the same pattern in pairs to explain the routes between these stations on the map. Stand up.

Victoria → Covent Garden
Covent Garden → Marble Arch
Marble Arch → Waterloo
Waterloo → Bank
Bank → Heathrow Central
Heathrow Central → somewhere else → somewhere else

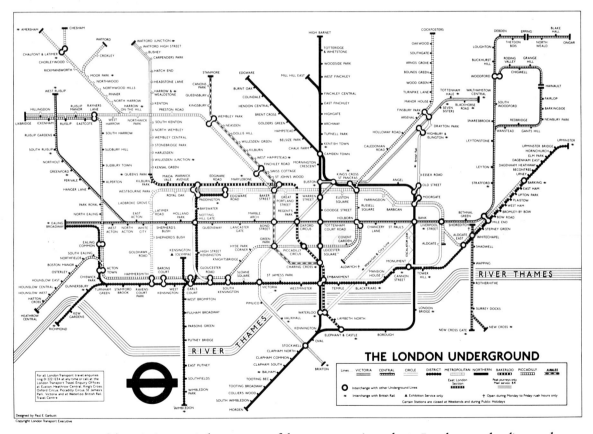

If there is time, switch to groups of three: one tourist and two Londoners who *disagree* about the best route!

## 9.6  Explaining timetables

Study this timetable for a few minutes – can you explain the symbols and abbreviations?

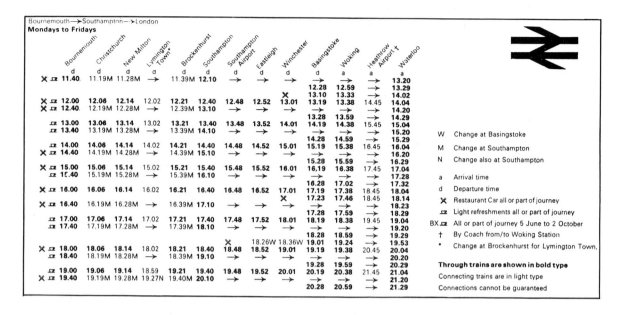

Bournemouth → Southampton → London
**Mondays to Fridays**

| | Bournemouth d | Christchurch d | New Milton d | Lymington Town d | Brockenhurst d | Southampton d | Southampton Airport d | Eastleigh d | Winchester d | Basingstoke d | Woking a | Heathrow Airport † a | Waterloo a |
|---|---|---|---|---|---|---|---|---|---|---|---|---|---|
| X ⊐ | 11.40 | 11.19M | 11.28M | → | 11.39M | 12.10 | → | → | → | → | → | → | 13.20 |
| | | | | | | | | | | 12.28 | 12.59 | → | 13.29 |
| | | | | | | | | | X 13.10 | 13.33 | → | | 14.02 |
| X ⊐ | 12.00 | 12.06 | 12.14 | 12.02 | 12.21 | 12.40 | 12.48 | 12.52 | 13.01 X | 13.19 | 13.38 | 14.45 | 14.04 |
| X ⊐ | 12.40 | 12.19M | 12.28M | → | 12.39M | 13.10 | → | → | → | → | → | → | 14.20 |
| | | | | | | | | | | 13.28 | 13.59 | → | 14.29 |
| ⊐ | 13.00 | 13.06 | 13.14 | 13.02 | 13.21 | 13.40 | 13.48 | 13.52 | 14.01 | 14.19 | 14.38 | 15.45 | 15.04 |
| ⊐ | 13.40 | 13.19M | 13.28M | → | 13.39M | 14.10 | → | → | → | → | → | → | 15.20 |
| | | | | | | | | | | 14.28 | 14.59 | → | 15.29 |
| X ⊐ | 14.00 | 14.06 | 14.14 | 14.02 | 14.21 | 14.40 | 14.48 | 14.52 | 15.01 | 15.19 | 15.38 | 16.45 | 16.04 |
| X ⊐ | 14.40 | 14.19M | 14.28M | → | 14.39M | 15.10 | → | → | → | → | → | → | 16.20 |
| | | | | | | | | | | 15.28 | 15.59 | → | 16.29 |
| X ⊐ | 15.00 | 15.06 | 15.14 | 15.02 | 15.21 | 15.40 | 15.48 | 15.52 | 16.01 | 16.19 | 16.38 | 17.45 | 17.04 |
| ⊐ | 15.40 | 15.19M | 15.28M | → | 15.39M | 16.10 | → | → | → | → | → | → | 17.28 |
| | | | | | | | | | | 16.28 | 17.02 | → | 17.32 |
| X ⊐ | 16.00 | 16.06 | 16.14 | 16.02 | 16.21 | 16.40 | 16.48 | 16.52 | 17.01 | 17.19 | 17.38 | 18.45 | 18.04 |
| | | | | | | | | | X 17.23 | 17.46 | 18.45 | | 18.14 |
| X ⊐ | 16.40 | 16.19M | 16.28M | → | 16.39M | 17.10 | → | → | → | → | → | → | 18.23 |
| | | | | | | | | | | 17.28 | 17.59 | → | 18.29 |
| ⊐ | 17.00 | 17.06 | 17.14 | 17.02 | 17.21 | 17.40 | 17.48 | 17.52 | 18.01 | 18.19 | 18.38 | 19.45 | 19.04 |
| ⊐ | 17.40 | 17.19M | 17.28M | → | 17.39M | 18.10 | → | → | → | → | → | → | 19.20 |
| | | | | | | | | | | 18.28 | 18.59 | → | 19.29 |
| | | | | | | | | X 18.26W | 18.36W | 19.01 | 19.24 | → | 19.53 |
| X ⊐ | 18.00 | 18.06 | 18.14 | 18.02 | 18.21 | 18.40 | 18.48 | 18.52 | 19.01 | 19.19 | 19.38 | 20.45 | 20.04 |
| ⊐ | 18.40 | 18.19M | 18.28M | → | 18.39M | 19.10 | → | → | → | → | → | → | 20.20 |
| | | | | | | | | | | 19.28 | 19.59 | → | 20.29 |
| ⊐ | 19.00 | 19.06 | 19.14 | 18.59 | 19.21 | 19.40 | 19.48 | 19.52 | 20.01 | 20.19 | 20.38 | 21.45 | 21.04 |
| X ⊐ | 19.40 | 19.19M | 19.28M | 19.27N | 19.40M | 20.10 | → | → | → | → | → | → | 21.20 |
| | | | | | | | | | | 20.28 | 20.59 | → | 21.29 |

W  Change at Basingstoke
M  Change at Southampton
N  Change also at Southampton
a  Arrival time
d  Departure time
X  Restaurant Car all or part of journey
⊐  Light refreshments all or part of journey
BX ⊐  All or part of journey 5 June to 2 October
†  By Coach from/to Woking Station
•  Change at Brockenhurst for Lymington Town.

**Through trains are shown in bold type**
Connecting trains are in light type
Connections cannot be guaranteed

*In pairs*  Advise these acquaintances how to get from Bournemouth to their destinations in good time.

A:  I've got a meeting in London at 2.20. The office is about ½ hour from Waterloo by tube.

B:  My flight leaves from Heathrow at 18.45.

C:  I'm meeting my sister in Southampton at 12.30.

D:  I'm flying from Southampton to le Touquet and then on to Paris. Check-in time is 13.40.

E:  I have to get to Basingstoke by 6 p.m.

F:  I want a fast train to London that'll get me there in time for the theatre.

G and H:  Invent your own requirements.

## 9.7  Discuss

# ⇌Inter-City makes the going easy

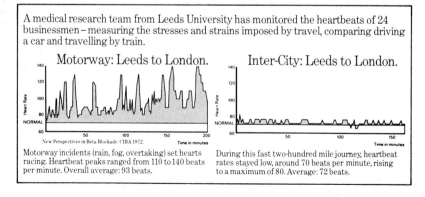

A medical research team from Leeds University has monitored the heartbeats of 24 businessmen – measuring the stresses and strains imposed by travel, comparing driving a car and travelling by train.

Motorway: Leeds to London.

New Perspectives in Beta Blockade: CIBA 1972.

Inter-City: Leeds to London.

Motorway incidents (rain, fog, overtaking) set hearts racing. Heartbeat peaks ranged from 110 to 140 beats per minute. Overall average: 93 beats.

During this fast two-hundred mile journey, heartbeat rates stayed low, around 70 beats per minute, rising to a maximum of 80. Average: 72 beats.

## 9.8 Game round the class: 'An imaginary journey'

Imagine you are about to go into a railway station. Give a running commentary of the things you do and see before, during and after your journey. Begin like this:
'I'm standing outside the station entrance and I'm just going to go inside and get my ticket from ...'

Your teacher will stop each speaker in mid-sentence and pass the commentary on to the next speaker.

Do the same with a bus journey, a car journey and, perhaps, a cycle ride.
Ask for the vocabulary you need!

## 9.9 Real journeys

*In small groups*  Tell the others about the last journey you made by train, by bus and by car.

## 9.10 Transportation: American English

Many terms are used to talk about transport in the United States that are not used in Britain. Can you 'translate' these American terms into British English:

| USA | GB |
|---|---|
| Gas/gasoline | petrol |
| gas pedal | |
| hood | |
| trunk | |
| fender | |
| a flat | |
| sedan | |
| station wagon | |
| truck | |
| streetcar | |
| cab | |
| bus | |
| trailer | |
| a one-way ticket | |
| a round trip ticket | |
| divided highway | |
| freeway | |
| turnpike | |
| sidewalk | |
| crosswalk | |
| pavement | |
| 'Can you give me a ride?' | |
| YIELD | |

Cover up the left-hand column and see if you (or your neighbour) can remember the American terms.

39

# 10 The future

Talking about future plans, arrangements and expectations
Predicting
Writing about future events in formal style
Expressing feelings about forthcoming events
Talking about simultaneous future activities

## 10.1 Plans and expectations

 A: What are you going to do *after this lesson*?
B: I'm | probably going to … | What about you?
        | planning to …
        | hoping to …
        | expecting to …
A: Oh, I'm …
B: I see.

Fill in the gaps in the conversation.

In pairs, follow the pattern to find out about each other's real plans and expectations at these times:

| | |
|---|---|
| When you get home | The day after tomorrow |
| At Christmas | In three days' time |
| On New Year's Eve | When we finish this conversation |
| This time next week | |

Report your findings to another pair.

## 10.2 Fixed arrangements

### 11 Tuesday

| | |
|---|---|
| 09.00 Mr. Green | 13.00 lunch with Brown |
| 9.30 Mr. Black | 14.00 interviews for |
| 10.00 Phone Amsterdam |       assistant manager |
| 10.30 see bank manager | 15.00 write reports |
| 11.00 Dentist | 16.00 Prepare documents for |
|     & do shopping – |       chairman |
| 12.00     birthday present | 17.00 see chairman |

40

A: Can you come and see me at 9 o'clock?
B: I'm afraid not, you see I'm meeting Mr Green at 9.

In pairs, continue the conversation through the day. Change roles overnight!

Think about what you have really arranged to do tomorrow. Tell the others.

## 10.3 Predicting

*In groups of three* One of you is a professional fortune-teller. The others have come to your tent for a consultation. In your crystal ball you can see the whole of your clients' lives spread out ahead. Begin like this:

'You will meet a stranger. He will be strangely fascinating. You will …'

When you have finished the consultation, change roles and tents. Make sure everyone gets a chance to be the fortune-teller.

*Talking point:* Have you ever visited a fortune-teller? Did the predictions come true?

## 10.4 Formal and informal style

Station announcement: 'The 9.40 train has been delayed and will not arrive at this station until 10.30 approximately.'

Telling a friend: 'There's been a delay and the train won't (*or* isn't going to) get in till about half past ten.'

Here are some more *formal* announcements. How would you tell a friend the same information?

'There will be showers in the London area and temperatures are expected to remain below normal.'

'The matinée performance will commence at 2.30 p.m. The part of Hamlet will be played for this performance only by Mr Michael Roberts.'

'The results of the June examinations will be published towards the end of September. Pass Certificates will be posted to successful candidates during November.'

'This train will terminate here. Passengers for the Weymouth line are requested to cross the footbridge to Platform 3, from which the connecting service will depart in seven minutes.'

41

'The goods you requested will be despatched by first-class post in ten days' time. We apologize for the delay and trust that you will not be inconvenienced.'

'We shall be obliged to take legal action if payment of our account is not made within seven days from the above date.'

'Due to unforeseen circumstances, the school will be closed until further notice.'

'During the summer season this store will be open from 7 p.m. to 9 p.m. each evening for the sale of books and magazines. The record department will remain closed.'

Now here are some very *informal* announcements.
In pairs, translate them into formal written English.

'It's going to rain tomorrow, but there might be a bit of sun.'

'The last bus normally goes at 11, but there's one at 11.30 on a Saturday.'

'Tomorrow's meeting's off – it's been put back to the same time next week.'

'The shops are going to be shut on Monday – it's a public holiday.'

'It's going to be a long hot July – a bit of rain at first, but pretty dry after that.'

'There's going to be a go-slow, so there aren't going to be any buses tomorrow morning.'

Read aloud what you have written to the rest of the class. Discuss the differences between each pair's versions.

## 10.5   It's about time ...

A: *It's about time I bought* the theatre tickets.
B: I know. When are you going to do it?
A: Oh ...  | Any minute now.
          | Very soon.
          | In a day or two.
          | In a few days' time.
          | Sometime soon.
          | One day.
          | As soon as I can.
          | When I get round to it.
B: Well, don't forget to buy them, will you?
A: I won't, don't worry.

*Don't Forget*

buy theatre tickets
get car serviced
write to Dad
phone Auntie
renew library books
holiday brochures
tidy office
paint hall
mow lawn
mend bike
take jacket to cleaners
get food for cats

In pairs, follow the same pattern to talk about the other things on the list.

Think of some real things that you have been meaning to do and tell the others.

## 10.6 Feelings about the future

A: I hear you're playing at a concert tomorrow. How do you feel about it?
B: Oh, I'm really | worried | about it.
| nervous
| anxious
| apprehensive |

or I'm really dreading it.
I'm quite confident about it.
I'm really looking forward to it.
I'm not that worried about it.
A: I'm not surprised. So would I be.
or Really? ↑

In pairs, follow the pattern to talk about these forthcoming events:

interview          dentist
exam               date
meeting            flight
party              wedding
holiday

Tell each other how you feel about what you're really going to do in the next few weeks.


## 10.7 Simultaneous activities

| B | A |
|---|---|
| wash up | breakfast in bed |
| clean living-room | walk in country |
| change bed-clothes | drink in pub |
| mow lawn | meal in restaurant |
| prepare dinner | talk to friends |
| write letters | go to theatre |
| feed cats | watch play |
| look after baby | visit night-clubs |
| do homework | dance |
| go to bed | watch floor-show |
| sleep | see sunrise |

A: What are your plans for tomorrow, Brenda?
B: Well, first I'm going to do the washing-up.
A: Poor you! While you're doing the washing-up, I'll be having breakfast in bed.
B: It's alright for some people.

In pairs, follow the pattern and go through the other activities in the same way.

Change partners but not roles and follow this pattern:

B: What are your plans for tomorrow, Arthur?
A: Well, first I'm going to have breakfast in bed.
B: You're lucky! While you're having breakfast in bed, I'll be doing the washing-up.
A: Well, someone has to do it, I suppose.

Talk about your real plans for this evening and tomorrow.

# 11 Speculating

Using conditional sentences accurately and appropriately

*A game in four rounds*

The class is divided into two teams, with the teacher as scorer and referee.
The aim is to score points for imagination, accuracy and appropriacy.
The game gets more difficult from round to round and the number of possible points goes up accordingly.

List of possible themes:

| work | prison | garden |
|------|--------|--------|
| holiday | shopping | cinema |
| interview | meal | wedding |
| journey | beach | London |
| plane | home | exam |

It is fairest for the referee to put these themes in a hat and draw them at random.

## 11.1 Round 1

| | |
|---|---|
| Referee prompts: | Team A: 'Work'. |
| Team A begins: | I'm going to work tomorrow. |
| Team B challenges: | What will you do if you're late? |
| *Score:* | *One point* |
| Team A answers: | If I'm late, I'll apologize! |
| *Score:* | *One point* |

Team A scores a point for an accurate reply to each question *and a bonus point* for each extra reply to the same question.

Team B continues challenging with more questions on the same theme scoring a point for each accurate question.

When Team B run out of questions, the referee prompts *them* to begin with a new theme.

Round 1 continues until the referee decides both teams are ready for Round 2. Team B are the last to speak. Count up the score.

## 11.2    Round 2

Referee prompts:      Team A: 'Prison'.
Team A begins:      I'm not in prison at the moment.
Team B challenges: What would you do if you were in prison?
*Score:*      *Two points: one for accuracy, one for good sense*
Team A answers:      If I were in prison, I'd feel unhappy.
*Score:*      *Two points: one for accuracy, one for good sense*

And so on, with two bonus points for each further reply to the questions.

Round 2 continues until the referee calls a halt. Team B must be the last to speak. Count up the score.

## 11.3    Round 3

Referee prompts:      Team A: 'Beach'.
Team A begins:      I didn't go to the beach yesterday.
Team B challenges: What would you have done if you had gone to the beach?
*Score:*      *Three points: one for accuracy in first half of sentence*
          *one for accuracy in second half of sentence*
          *one for good sense*
Team A answers:      If I'd gone to the beach, I'd have gone swimming.
*Score:*      *Three points: as above*

And so on with three bonus points for each further reply to the questions. Team B is the last to speak. Count up the score.

## 11.4    Round 4: in the next lesson

Referee prompts:      Team A: 'Beach'.
Team A has a choice of: I'm going to the beach tomorrow.
          *or:*  I'm not at the beach at the moment.
          *or:*  I didn't go to the beach yesterday.

Team B challenges according to the choice A made, scoring three points for accuracy and following the choice correctly, and one for good sense.

Team A replies, again scoring up to four points.

NO bonus points in this round.

Count up the score and declare the winners!

## 11.5    'Visit the USA!'

*In three groups*  Look at the map of the USA on page 46.

Group A: If you can afford it, you are going to visit the USA next summer. If you do go, where exactly will you go? What will you see? How will you travel?

Decide on your reasons for each choice.

Group B: There's no chance of your visiting the USA next summer – you simply can't afford it. But it's nice to dream! If you could afford to go, where exactly would you go? What would you see?
How would you travel?
Decide on your reasons for each choice.

Group C: You didn't go to the USA last summer. But suppose you had gone there, where exactly would you have gone? What would you have seen? How would you have travelled?
Decide on your reasons for each choice.

When each group is ready with its plans or dreams, the class is divided up into smaller groups. Each small group should consist of at least one member of Groups A, B and C. Report what your group talked about and discuss the reasons.

If there is time, the activity can be repeated with a visit to Asia and a visit to Latin America. Students should go back to their original groups but change their letter (Group A becomes Group B and so on). In this way each group will practise different forms.

## 12 Home

Talking about houses, flats and household equipment

### 12.1 Can you use these words?

| | | |
|---|---|---|
| detached | mortgage | caretaker |
| semi-detached | rent | daily help |
| terrace | rates | householder |
| bungalow | | landlord |
| block of flats | | tenant |

### 12.2 Your own home

*In groups*   Draw the house or flat you live in and label the parts.

| | | |
|---|---|---|
| | | |
| Front view | Plan of Ground Floor | Plan of First Floor |

Tell the others in the group about its appearance and what it contains. Make sure you can put a name to all the furniture and equipment in each room.

Ask your teacher for vocabulary when you need it.

### 12.3 'Redevelopment'

*In groups*   You each have a flat in a large old building which is about to be demolished by the local council. As part of the redevelopment scheme, you are to be rehoused in a small block of flats on a site opposite this school. You have the opportunity to state your views on the new building:

You can plan two-bedroom flats – how should they be designed and equipped? On the ground floor there is room for two commercial premises – would you prefer shops, restaurant, bar, café? If shops, what type? Remember that the flats are opposite this school.

1 Discuss your ideas and make notes of the decisions you make.
2 Report your plans to the other groups.
3 Write a report to the local authority.

### 12.4 'Ideal home'

Draw a sketch plan of your ideal living/dining-room. Write a description of it. Make it really the best living area you can imagine! What would the other rooms be like?

### 12.5 Talking point: Changes in homes this century

*In groups*  Begin like this: 'We take … for granted, but 100 years ago people used to …'

Use the same pattern to talk about TV, washing machines, telephones, central heating, running water, electrical appliances, etc.

### 12.6 Labour-saving devices

Describe the way this dining-room set-up works:

In groups design a labour-saving device of your own to cut down on or eliminate housework or kitchen chores, to answer the telephone or to deal with unwelcome callers. Each group reports its invention to the other groups later – a diagram on the board will help here!

## 12.7 Game: 'Finding somewhere to live'

The class is divided into two groups: one half looking for accommodation, the other half with houses, flats or rooms to let. Each person writes an advertisement describing exactly what he personally needs or has to offer.

The idea of the game is to find the right tenant and the right accommodation. Each prospective tenant goes from landlord to landlord, showing his own advertisement and reading the landlord's. When eventually a reasonably suitable 'match' is found, negotiate the rent and conditions.

Here, for example, are two advertisements that *don't* match:

"Young couple with 3 children seek large
house for 3 months, preferably central.
Any offers considered."

"Country cottage, 2 bedrooms, to let.
Very secluded position. No dogs or
children. Long-term lease only.
Harris, "Belinda Cottage", Talbot Woods".

## 13 Ability

Talking about ability and inability

### 13.1 Present and future time

| + | − | ? |
|---|---|---|
| He's capable of … | He's incapable of … | Is he capable of …? |
| He can … | He can't … | Can he …? |
| He's able to … | He's unable to … | Is he able to …? |
| He knows how to … | He doesn't know how to … | Does he know how to …? |
| He'll be able to … | He won't be able to … | Will he be able to …? |
| He could … | He'd be unable to … | |
| (but he might not) | | |

Discuss when you would use each form.
Cover up each column of the chart and remember the words.
Finish off each sentence.

### 13.2 What can you do?

*In groups*  Talk about your own abilities, skills and talents.
Ask each other questions about:

swimming
languages
sports
card games
board games
photography
driving
do-it-yourself
cooking

Future abilities may depend on training, time available and other commitments. Imagine you are attending evening classes on some things you can't do now. At the end of term how will your abilities be different? Ask each other questions.

Think about the coming weekend. Ask each other what you will be able to do, and what you won't be able to do and why not.

### 13.3 Past time

| **+** | **−** | **?** |
|---|---|---|
| He was able to … | He wasn't able to … | Was he able to …? |
| He managed to … | He didn't manage to … | Did he manage to …? |
| He could have … | He couldn't … | |
| (but he didn't) | | |

! *REMEMBER* ! that 'he could do it when he was young' is only used in sentences like these:

He could | play the piano.
⎪ swim.
⎪ read and write.
NOT: He could go to the cinema.
He could catch the bus.

Discuss when you would use each form.
Cover up each column and remember the words.
Finish off each sentence.


### 13.4 What were you able to do?

*In groups*  When you were a child, at what age could you do these things? Ask each other:

| | | |
|---|---|---|
| talk | feed yourself | ride a bike |
| read | dress yourself | play football |
| write | swim | play a musical instrument |

Last weekend what were you able to do? And what couldn't you do? Ask each other.

# 14 Money

Being a customer in a bank
Talking about personal financial affairs

## 14.1 In a bank

| | | |
|---|---|---|
| Customer: | I'd like to ... | *Request* |
| Cashier: | Certainly, would you please ... | *Reaction* |
| Customer: | Oh yes. There you are. | |
| Cashier: | How would you like the money? | *Continuation* |
| Customer: | In fives, please. | |
| Cashier: | Fine. Here you are. | |
| Customer: | Thanks. Goodbye. | |

Can you use these phrases in the conversation?

pay this into my current account/deposit account    *Requests*
withdraw £— from my ...
cash this cheque/travellers cheque

show me your cheque card/passport    *Reactions*
sign it/initial it
put the name of the payee/the date

In pairs, act out the situation. Change roles.

## 14.2 The past week's expenses

Useful language

I spent £— on ...                The bill came to £—
... cost £—                      I paid £— for ...
It all came to £—                I bought ... for £—

*In groups*  Talk about all the money you have spent in the past week. What was the expenditure you resented most. What was the most worthwhile expenditure?

## 14.3 Winning the pools

*In groups*  It is Saturday afternoon and you have just heard the football results and found out that one of you has probably won several thousand pounds on the pools. Work out a plan of how to spend or invest the money.

Report your plan to the other groups.

### 14.4 Your own finances

*In groups*  Talk about how often you use these facilities. If you don't use them, why don't you? Do you disapprove of them?

credit cards                          personal loan from a bank
pawnshop                             overdraft
cheque book                          borrowing from a friend or relation
travellers cheques                   grant or scholarship
hire purchase                        unemployment benefit

### 14.5 Other people's money

Especially when talking about other people we use expressions like these:

He's | finding it hard to make ends meet
     | broke
     | in debt
     | hard up
     | comfortably off
     | in the money
     | making a fortune
     | stinking rich

What other expressions can be used to describe other people's wealth?

Use the expressions to describe these people.
Give examples of what each person can and can't afford.

### 14.6  A budget meeting

*In groups*  You have a budget of £10,000 to spend on educational and social improvements to the facilities of your school or college. Make a list of the suggestions made. Decide on your priorities and estimate how much each idea would cost. Repeat your decisions to the class when you have finished.

Useful language

It's not worth spending £— on …
It'd be better to spend £— on …
Are you sure we can afford to …?
It wouldn't be fair to …
Have you any idea how much … would cost?
That'd cost something in the region of £—


### 14.7  Debate: 'Money causes more problems than it solves'

The day before decide who is going to be:

Chairman
Proposer (first speaker *for* the motion)
Second and third speakers *for* the motion
Opposer (first speaker *against* the motion)
Second and third speakers *against* the motion

Speakers should prepare their speeches in note form. Speeches should be biased *for* or *against*, not present a balanced view!

On the day, the speakers make their speeches one by one in this order:
Proposer
Opposer
Second speaker *for*
Second speaker *against*
Third speaker *for*
Third speaker *against*

Then the discussion is open to the floor, for everyone else to state their views. Finally, the proposer and opposer sum up and a vote is taken *for* or *against* the motion.

# 15 Place

Describing spatial relationships

## 15.1 Exact positions

What prepositions or prepositional phrases would describe the position of each letter?
For example: 'A is inside the left-hand box – quite near the bottom left-hand corner of it.'

Add two more letters each and tell the other students where you have put them.

Secretly draw your own diagram with the letters M to Z scattered around inside and outside the two boxes. Then, in pairs, get your partner to draw *your* diagram telling him where exactly to put each letter. Then draw *his* diagram according to his directions.

! *CAREFUL* ! how you use 'left' and 'right'.
We say: *on the left* and *on the left-hand side*
(but NOT: on the left side)

## 15.2 Places you do things

Where do you normally do or buy these things?

| | | | |
|---|---|---|---|
| sleep | play football | buy stamps | go for a walk |
| watch TV | tennis | fruit | drive |
| eat | golf | meat | swim |
| comb your hair | | books | cup of tea |
| cut your nails | | nails | |
| | | wine | |

Be as precise as possible!

## 15.3 Places: on a page

There are fifteen dots scattered about this page. Where exactly are they all?
Cross off each one as it is identified by one of the group ●

### 15.4 Game: 'Places in a room'

Think of an object that is somewhere in the room. Be prepared to answer questions from everyone else about where it is. You can only answer 'Yes' or 'No'.

### 15.5 Place: in relation to people

Look at the photograph. The ball might be in several different places – how would you describe each possible place?

### 15.6 'Picture dictation'

*In groups*    Each member of the group secretly draws a picture of a country scene, group of people or town scene. Then each member explains to the others how to draw his scene *without* showing them the original. Then compare the results. Use a fresh sheet of paper for each picture.

# 16 Health

Inquiring about health as an initiating gambit and responding
Describing your own and others' health
Talking about medical facilities

## 16.1 How are you?

When someone asks you how you are, they often don't expect a detailed medical report. They usually expect a response like:

 Fine, thanks – and you?
Very well thanks.
Oh, not too bad, you know.
Oh, mustn't grumble, you know.
Much better, thanks.

In pairs, practise using these responses.

## 16.2 Can you use these words?

| | | | |
|---|---|---|---|
| family doctor | temperature | tablets | surgery |
| midwife | infection | medicine | ward |
| surgeon | bug | thermometer | clinic |
| specialist | pain | prescription | operating theatre |
| receptionist | soreness | | |
| patient | ache | | |
| hypochondriac | spots | | |
| | rash | | |

Can you label the parts of the body?
Get your teacher or one of the class to stand up and label the parts of his or her body. Then do the same in pairs with your own bodies. What can go wrong with each part?

## 16.3 Medical problems

 Useful language

How are you feeling?
You don't look very well.
Are you alright?
What's the matter?

We can answer these questions in several ways. Typically, we might want to make light of our ailments or exaggerate them. Fill in the gaps:

| | *Mild* | *Extreme* |
|---|---|---|
| | I feel a bit off colour. | I think I'm dying. |
| | I feel a bit under the weather. | I feel absolutely rotten. |
| headache | I've got a bit of a headache. | I've got a … headache. |
| backache | My back's giving me a bit of trouble. | My back's … |
| feeling sick | I feel a bit … | I think I'm going to … |
| sore throat | My throat's a bit dry. | I can hardly … |
| cough | I've got a … in my throat. | I can't … |
| stiffness | I'm … | I can't move. |
| catarrh | I'm a bit stuffed up. | I … |
| insomnia | I'm having a bit of trouble sleeping. | I didn't … last night. |
| toothache | This tooth's playing up a bit. | … |
| chest pains | My chest … | I've got … in my chest. |

Cover up each column and remember the sentences.

Follow this pattern conversation and use the expressions above:

A: How are you, Brenda?
B: Fine, apart from …
A: Oh dear, I'm sorry to hear that.
B: Yes … (*mild or extreme description*)
A: Well, I hope you soon feel better!
*or* Let's hope you soon get over it!
B: Thanks!

## 16.4 Illnesses and accidents

What are the symptoms of:

| | |
|---|---|
| flu | sunstroke |
| a cold | food poisoning |
| rheumatism | a hangover |
| bronchitis | |

In pairs (sitting back-to-back so you can't see each other) improvise a series of telephone conversations between yourself and the doctor's receptionist. The problem is that your friend is ill in bed and you want the doctor to visit him at home. Use some of these expressions:

| | |
|---|---|
| Hallo, is that …? | What are the symptoms? |
| My name's … | It sounds like … |
| I'm ringing on behalf of … | It could be a case of … |
| Could Dr Bones come and have a look at him, please? | I'll get the doctor to … |
| | Can't your friend come to the surgery? |

Your friend has flu one day, sunstroke the next, then food poisoning, then he has been stung by a swarm of bees, then fallen off a ladder.

**Fire**
**Police**
**Ambulance**

**Coastguard**
**Lifeboat**
**Rescue**

**Call the Operator**
**by dialling 999**

or as shown on your dial label or dialling instructions

Tell the operator the service you want.

Give your exchange and number or all-figure number as appropriate

Wait until the Emergency authority answers

Then give them the full address where help is needed and other necessary information

How do you call an ambulance in your country?

**16.6    Talking point: your country**

Are medical services free in your country?
How is the system organized in your country?

**16.7    Talking points**

*In groups*    How do you stay healthy and fit?
What sort of exercise do you take?
Do you play any sports?
Do you do yoga?
Do you do keep-fit exercises?
Do you jog?
What do you think of people who do?

Report the results of your discussion to the other groups.

## 17 Passive

Describing actions when the agent is unknown or unimportant
Using passives in impersonal style

### 17.1 'Who by?' 'I don't know'

A: Where's the letter?
B: It's being typed right now.
A: Who by?
B: Oh, I don't know. Someone in the typing pool, I suppose.

In pairs, follow the pattern using these prompts:

car – repair
coat – clean
socks – wash
TV – fix
homework – mark
house – clean

Use the same prompts to follow this pattern:

A: What a well laid-out letter!
B: Yes, it's just been typed, actually.
A: Who by?
B: I'm not sure, but whoever it was, they've made a good job of it.
A: They certainly have!

### 17.2 Sherlock Holmes

Watson: How do you think he was killed, Holmes?
Holmes: There's no doubt he was shot, Watson.
Watson: But how do you know?
Holmes: He must have been shot, my dear Watson,
there's the gun he was shot with.
Watson: You're a brilliant man, Holmes!

*In pairs* Follow the same pattern to talk about these murder weapons and causes of death:

knife
arsenic
rope
pillow
!*bath*!
!*tiger*!

## 17.3  Guessing causes

Little Sally, age 9, is crying. Why?

She | might | have been | told off.
| could | | smacked.
| | | frightened.
| | | sent to bed early.

*In groups*  Now guess the causes of these events:

There's a man running down the road.
There's a dog barking.
Mary, age 17, is blushing.
There's a car in the river.
The window's smashed.
John looks very happy after opening that letter.

Report the best theories to the other groups.

## 17.4  Getting attention away from the agent

A: I'm afraid your window has got broken.
B: Who was it broken by?
A: Me – but it wasn't my fault!
B: How did it happen?
A: Well … (*cause*)

*In pairs*  Follow the same pattern, using these prompts:

lost key
damaged car
eaten cakes
empty whisky bottle
torn newspaper
book written in
letter opened

61

## 17.5 Impersonal style: in written reports

 'Well, we put the powder into the liquid and then let it dissolve.'

The powder was placed in the liquid and allowed to dissolve.

'Anyway, they managed to get to the summit on May 1st.'

The summit was reached on May 1st.

In pairs, transform these informal spoken accounts into written report style:

'It was ever such a strong wind – it blew down about a dozen trees, you know.'

'They got away with over £10,000 when they robbed the bank.'

'We put what was in the bottle into a glass of water.'

'We sent them the money right away.'

'I'm afraid I opened your letter by mistake.'

'There was all that rain, you see and it washed away the railway track.'

'So the boss sent for him and told him to collect his cards.'

'He took the pills and he got better.'

Discuss your sentences with the other groups.

## 17.6 What has to be done

*In groups*  Think of all the things that have to be done or can be done before you:

move into a new flat
get married
go on holiday
have a meal

Report to the other groups.

## 17.7 Team game: 'Transformation'

Team A challenges Team B to transform a sentence from active to passive. Team B scores a point for accuracy. If they fail to answer or respond inaccurately, Team A can themselves score a bonus point if they can transform the sentence accurately.
Teams take it in turns to challenge. The game can be in four rounds: past time, present time, future time and mixed times, if required.

## 18 Motion

Describing motion
Describing directions

### 18.1 Direction: appropriate prepositions

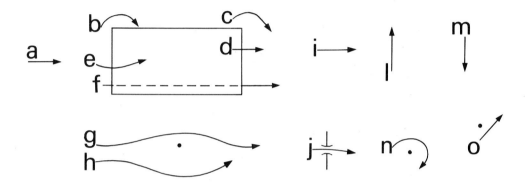

What prepositions or prepositional phrases describe the direction of movement of each letter in the diagram? For example, A is 'moving towards the box'.

### 18.2 Describing motion: verbs and prepositional phrases

He ran = he went (or came) very fast on foot.
He flew = he went (or came) by plane.

Explain or demonstrate what these verbs of motion mean:

| | |
|---|---|
| He drove | He crept |
| He cycled | He fell |
| He sailed | He slid |
| He walked | He bent |
| He rode | He tiptoed |
| He crawled | He hopped |
| He marched | He limped |
| He strolled | He shuffled |
| He rushed | He jumped |
| He dashed | |

Make notes of the explanation of each verb, then cover up each column and remember the verbs.

### 18.3 Exercise

*In pairs*   Make a complete sentence from each of these openings, using an appropriate verb or prepositional phrase of motion:

The soldiers …         The injured player …
The cat …              The late student …
The mouse …            The ship …
The glass …            The little boy …
The snake …

Discuss your sentences with the rest of the class.


### 18.4 Describing motion: transitive verbs of motion

Demonstrate what each of these verbs means:

He threw it            He took it
He dropped it          He brought it
He picked it up        He fetched it
He pulled it           He moved it
He pushed it           He shifted it
He lowered it          He lifted it
He raised it           He put it down

In pairs, mime each of the above actions in mixed order. Get your partner to say what you're doing.


### 18.5 Describing motion: adverbial particles

Demonstrate these sentences:

He walked off *or* He walked away.         He walked across.
He walked past.                            He walked round.
He walked in.                              He walked along.
He walked out.                             He walked up and down.
He walked on.                              He walked round and round.


### 18.6 Exercise

*In pairs*   Make a complete sentence from each of these openings, using an appropriate verb of motion:

The pan was hot, so …                  Waiter, I haven't finished my soup, …
The shop was closed, so …              I was bored, so …
He saw the ghost and …                 I'd finished reading, so …
He fell into the lake, so …            I couldn't understand the exam paper, so …
His new watch didn't work, so …        I've left my coat outside, could you …

### 18.7 Direction: routes in the town

Get a map of the town or city you are living in (or draw a sketch map). Without pointing, describe your route to school from home. The others follow the route and can ask questions on the way.

Now explain the best route to the:

| | |
|---|---|
| best restaurant in town | railway station |
| best store in town | bus station |
| police station | river or sea |

Now make up a 'surprise route' to somewhere else from this room. The others should try to guess where you're heading.

### 18.8 Directions

*In small groups*  Describe in detail the route you would take from here to:

| | |
|---|---|
| Paris | Cambridge |
| New York | Sydney |
| Rome | Hong Kong |

### 18.9 'Jumbo': a problem to solve

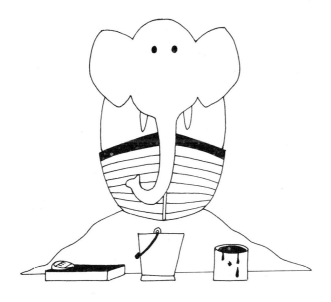

*In pairs or small groups*  You want to find out the weight of your elephant.
You have:

| | |
|---|---|
| a large pile of sand | some paint |
| a set of bathroom scales | a boat |
| a bucket | |

Work out how to weigh the elephant and then each write down your method.

# 19 Possibility

Talking about possibility and impossibility

## 19.1 Present and future time

| + | — | ? |
|---|---|---|
| It's possible that he ... | It's impossible that he ... | Is it possible that he ...? |
| He may ... | He can't ... | Could he ...? |
| He might ... | He couldn't ... | Might he ...? |
| He could ... | I'm sure he isn't ... | Is he perhaps ...? |
| Possibly he ... | He certainly doesn't ... | Does he perhaps ...? |
| Perhaps he ... | He definitely won't ... | Will he perhaps ...? |

! *REMEMBER* ! that   He may not ... He might not ...   do not refer to *im*possibility.
(He must be ... = It's probable that he ...)

Discuss when you would use each form.
Cover up each column and remember the words.
Finish off each sentence.

## 19.2 Guess!

*In groups*   Collect some magazine pictures and ask each other questions about them. Try to imagine all the possible interpretations and implications.

Think about people you know who are not present at the moment. What are they doing? For example, your parents, relations, friends, famous people, other teachers and students.

Talk about next week. What might happen in the world? What might happen in your life?

## 19.3 Past time

| + | — | ? |
|---|---|---|
| He may have ... | He can't have ... | Could he have ...? |
| He might have ... | He couldn't have ... | Might he have ...? |
| He could have ... | I'm sure he wasn't ... | Did he perhaps ...? |
| Possible he ... | He certainly didn't ... | Was he perhaps ...? |
| Perhaps he ... | | |

(He must have ... = It's probable that he ...)

Discuss when you would use each form.
Cover up each column and remember the words.
Finish off each sentence.

### 19.4 Guess why!

Here are some events. Can you suggest their causes?

Michael is bankrupt.  Belinda has bought a Rolls-Royce.
John has a hangover.  Chris flew to Rio suddenly.
Sue feels sick.  Peter is very tired.
Perry is depressed.  Rachel has a pain in her back.
Rob is very happy.  Leo is very very worried.

### 19.5 Guess what!

*In groups*   Can you guess what the others in your group were doing at different times of day last Sunday? And this time last year?

### 19.6 A story

*In groups (or as a whole class)*   Suggest answers to the questions in this story. Decide which is the best suggestion made.

'Our hero (*guess who?*) got up (*guess when?*) and had breakfast (*what?*) and travelled (*how?*) to somewhere (*where?*). On his arrival he did something (*what?*) to another person (*who?*) and they both did something (*what?*). For a long time they discussed something (*what?*), then they made a decision (*what?*). Someone else (*who?*) arrived and said something (*what?*) to them. Very quickly our hero did something (*what?*) and went on another journey (*where to?*) with someone else (*guess who?*). This whole affair was reported in the newspaper under an eye-catching headline (*what?*).

Tell your story to the other groups. Give the headline first.

# 20 Spelling

Spelling and pronouncing vowel and diphthong sounds accurately
Pronouncing English names accurately
Pronouncing words distinguished by word-stress accurately

## 20.1 Vowels and diphthongs

Here are examples of the important spelling rules for English vowel and diphthong sounds.
Sometimes there are two or more spellings of words that are pronounced the same.
Look at the lists before the lesson and look up the words you don't know.

| | | | |
|---|---|---|---|
| sheep | ship | head | bear + bare |
| key | biscuit | when | where + wear |
| read + reed | enjoy | read + red | stare + stair |
| queen | dishes | friend | mayor + mare |
| piece + peace | wicked | said | prayer |
| ceiling | modest | many | air + heir |
| sealing | kitchen | bury + berry | tear |
| seize + seas | necklace | says | share |
| receive | banquet | leisure | scarce |
| people | palace | pleasure | hair + hare |
| grief | mystery | threat | |
| weak + week | college | breath | |
| believe | marriage | whether + weather | |
| | guilty | | |
| | business | | |
| | bargain | | hut — London |
| | witch + which | | fun — flourish |

tongue — blood
month — monkey
country — glove
flood
onion
worry
enough
money

cat
hand
plaits

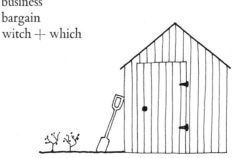

castle
father
guard
laugh
clerk + Clarke
heart
half
can't
Derby
drama
draught + draft

dog
what + watt
yacht
cross
cauliflower
cough
sausage
knowledge
because
Austria
orange
squash
quality

yawn
more
war + wore
abroad
shore + sure + Shaw
law
caught + court
George
bald
floor
source + sauce
laundry
sword + sawed

whale + wail
say
ate + eight
chamber
break + brake
ache
gauge
angel
jail
wait + weight
obey

goat
comb
folk
whole + hole
brooch
glow
soul + sole
so + sew + sow
coal
bow

bull
book
pull
wolf
should
butcher
bullet
cushion
push
woolly
bush
bosom
pussy
pudding

boots
who
move
true
youth
tomb
wound
threw + through
loose
lose
truth
nuisance
refuse
Hugh
Sue

bird
turn
heard + herd
work
journey
firm
worm
colonel + kernel
sir
learn
curly
word
fur + fir

bike
why
height
high
guide
eye + I
mind + mined
isle + aisle + I'll
climb it + climate
guy
reply
thigh
die + dye

cow
owl
foul
plough
drown
crowd
bow + bough

boy
oyster
destroy
point

deer + dear
hear + here
pioneer
clear
fear

## 20.2 More words

Add these words to the appropriate lists on pages 68 or 69:

| | |
|---|---|
| treasure | paper |
| foreign | early |
| hypocrite | honey |
| beard | leather |
| ball | dirty |
| woke | sandwich |
| fright | veal |
| freight | beef |

## 20.3 Game: 'Definitions'

*In pairs or threes*   Ask each other questions about the words in 20.1:

'What does "…" mean?'
'What's the difference between "…" and "…"?'

And answer like this:

'A "…" is something/someone … .'
*or* 'When you "…" something/someone, you … .'
*or* 'A "…" is the same as a … .'
*or* Draw a picture or do a mime.

Score a point for a correct answer.

## 20.4 Spelling game

*In pairs or teams*   Challenge each other to a spelling competition. Say a word from the lists in 20.1 and get your opponent to spell it aloud. Do this first column by column. Then start jumping about!

## 20.5 Pronouncing names

Pronounce the names of these couples correctly in English:

Herbert and Elizabeth Clarke
Edward and Alice Mackenzie
Keith and Daphne Johnson
Anthony and Hilary Tyler
Derek and Jane Baker
Arthur and Janet Thompson
Nigel and Laura Richardson
Gerald and Patricia Hughes
Jeremy and Penelope Chambers
Ralph and Rachel Bush
Timothy and Rosemary Leadbetter
Maurice and Virginia O'Neill

In groups, look at any page of a British Telephone Directory. Can you read aloud the names, addresses and telephone numbers of ten different people on the page?

Privately, make a list of the British people you know personally. Then see if the others in your group can pronounce them correctly.

What are the 'short' Christian names used for the people you have mentioned? Begin with the people in the list above: For example:
'Herbert is called "Bert" for short; Elizabeth is called "Liz" for short; "Alice" doesn't usually have a short form …'

And about your British acquaintances: 'My friend Tom's full name is "Thomas" and your friend Sue's full name is "Susan" …'

## 20.6 Word-stress

Here are some words which are spelt the same but pronounced differently:

record: an LP *record* / we re*cor*ded their voices
perfect: a *per*fect crime / I have per*fec*ted a new method

In groups, work out examples of each pronunciation of these words. Then report your examples to the other groups:

| | |
|---|---|
| to suspect | a suspect |
| to separate | a separate amount |
| to permit | a permit |
| to progress | his progress |
| to protest | a protest |
| to insult | an insult |

*Different meanings:*

| | | |
|---|---|---|
| to contract | a contract | |
| to conduct | his conduct | |
| to subject | a subject | |
| to desert | a desert | (a dessert) |
| a minute's wait | a minute quantity | |
| to object | an object | |

# 21 Feelings

Describing your own and others' feelings, moods, facial expressions and gestures

## 21.1 Happy?

A: How do you feel?
B: I'm ...

Add more expressions for each picture:

| cheerful | fed up | in a bad temper | nervous |

In groups, make a list of the things that make you | happy
unhappy
angry
nervous.

Then report your list, item by item, to the others like this:

Group member A: When do you feel cheerful, B?
Group member B: When ...
Group member C: What puts you in a good mood, D?
Group member D: *Replies with the next item from the list.*

What other moods can you be in?

## 21.2 Appearances

*In pairs* A: You | sound a bit *sad or* very *happy*.
look a bit *angry*.
seem a bit *nervous*.
B: Well, you see ... (*reason*)
A: Oh, what happened exactly?
B: Well ... (*details*)

Follow the pattern, taking feelings from 21.1 and reasons from the list below:

| | |
|---|---|
| lost wallet | been insulted |
| got engaged | had shock |
| car stolen | passed exam |
| got headache | car damaged |
| fallen in love | missed bus |

## 21.3  Expressions and gestures

Demonstrate these words:

| with a | sneer | sigh | laugh |
|---|---|---|---|
| | shrug | cough | giggle |
| | wave | sneeze | chuckle |
| | wink | groan | snigger |
| | blink | moan | smile |
| | scowl | hiccup | grin |
| | frown | yawn | |
| | | gasp | |
| | | whistle | |
| | | scream | |
| | | sniff | |
| | | sob | |

In pairs or groups, demonstrate the expressions and gestures in mixed order and put the right name to each one.

## 21.4  More feelings and tone of voice

Say 'Oh' in different ways to express these feelings:

| | |
|---|---|
| surprise | being impressed |
| astonishment | despair |
| fright | sympathy |
| disappointment | lack of interest |
| anger | disbelief |
| pain | nervousness |

In pairs, say 'Oh' in various ways and get your partner to identify the feeling you are demonstrating like this:

A: Oh!
B: You sound as if you …

Here are some more ways of expressing feelings. Put them with the appropriate feeling in the list above. Some may go with more than one feeling.

| | | | |
|---|---|---|---|
| Fancy that! | Good heavens! | Very good indeed! | Oh dear! |
| Well, well, well! | I can't stand it! | My God! | You don't say! |
| I see! | Well done! | Oh no! | What a shame! |
| What a nuisance! | Congratulations! | My goodness! | |

In pairs, write remarks to which 'Oh' or one of the above exclamations might be the reply. For example:

A: I've failed my exam.
B: What a shame! *or* Oh!

Act out your mini-dialogues.

!\*CAREFUL\*! about your tone of voice.

## 22 Permission and obligation

Talking about permission and prohibition
Talking about obligation and necessity

### 22.1 Permission: present and future time

| + | − | ? |
|---|---|---|
| He is allowed to ... | He is not allowed to ... | Is he allowed to ...? |
| He will be allowed to ... | He won't be allowed to ... | Will he be allowed to ...? |
| He can ... | He can't ... | Can he ...? |
| He may ... | He mustn't ... | May he ...? |
| He is permitted to ... | He hasn't to ... | Could he ...? |
| | He shouldn't ... | Is he permitted to ...? |
| | He isn't supposed to ... | |
| | He isn't permitted to ... | |

! *NOTICE* ! that 'He could do it' implies that he is allowed to do it but probably *won't*.

Discuss when you would use each form.
Cover up each column and remember the words.
Finish off each sentence.

### 22.2 What can you do?

Think of a game or sport you are all familiar with. Make some notes. What are the rules? What can you do and what can't you do? (What do you have to do?)

Children and teenagers these days have a lot more freedom now than they used to. What can they do? What can't they do that adults can?

### 22.3 Permission: past time

| + | − | ? |
|---|---|---|
| He was allowed to ... | He wasn't allowed to ... | Was he allowed to ...? |
| He was able to ... | He couldn't ... | Could he ...? |
| He could ... | He wasn't able to ... | Was he able to ...? |
| He had permission to ... | He didn't have permission to ... | Did he have permission to ...? |

! *NOTICE* ! the implications of these forms:

He could have ...   implies that he was allowed to but *didn't* do it.
He should have ... / He wasn't supposed to ...   imply that he wasn't allowed to but *did* do it.

Discuss when you would use each form.
Cover up each column and remember the forms.
Finish off each sentence.

## 22.4 Your past

Think of your own childhood. What couldn't you do then that you can do now? What did you have to do? Did you always do what you were supposed to do? At school, what did you have to ask permission to do? What weren't you allowed to do?

## 22.5 Obligation: present and future time

| + | − | ? |
|---|---|---|
| He must … | He needn't … | Must he …? |
| He has to … | He doesn't have to … | Does he have to …? |
| He ought to … | He doesn't need to … | Does he need to …? |
| He should … | There's no need for him to … | Should he …? |
| He's supposed to … | It isn't compulsory | Ought he to …? |
| He needs to … | It's optional | Is he supposed to …? |
| It's compulsory | It's unnecessary for him to … | Is it compulsory? |
| It's necessary for him to … | | Is it optional? |
| | | Is it necessary for him to …? |

Discuss when you would use each form.
Cover up each column and remember the forms.
Finish off each sentence.

## 22.6

*Sea View Guest House*

(Proprietor : Mrs Rose Gubbins)

RULES OF THE HOUSE

No Smoking
Breakfast at 8.30 a.m. sharp
Dinner at 6 p.m. sharp
No alcoholic drinks
No dogs
No visitors after 8 p.m.
Visitors in the lounge <u>only</u>
No loud music in rooms
Baths – 50p
Rooms to be vacated from
    10 a.m. to 5 p.m.

*In groups*  Add two more rules.

Choose one of these roles:

Mrs Gubbins
a nervous new guest
the polite Mr Gubbins
a regular law-abiding guest
a regular anti-authoritarian guest

(Add more guests or staff for a larger group.)

Move your chairs to represent two separate rooms. Plan a series of scenes that might take place at Sea View. Act them out for the other groups.

## 22.7  In Britain

*In groups*  Imagine you are talking to a group of foreigners who have never left their own country. What would you tell them about the rules of social behaviour in Britain? Make notes and report your rules to the other groups.

## 22.8  Obligation: past time

| **+** | **−** | **?** |
|---|---|---|
| He had to … | He didn't need to … | Did he have to …? |
| It was compulsory | It was optional | Did he need to …? |
| He had no choice but to … | There was no need to … | Was it compulsory? |

! *NOTICE* ! the implications of these forms:

He should have … /He was supposed to …   imply that it was compulsory, but he *didn't* do it.
He needn't have … /He didn't have to …   imply that it was not compulsory, but he *did* do it.

Discuss when you would use each form.
Cover up each column and remember the forms.
Finish off each sentence.

## 22.9  Utopia?

*In groups*  1 You are citizens of a newly independent state called Utopia. Draft a set of laws to give everyone as much freedom as possible. Make notes and tell the other groups what they will and won't be allowed to do in *your* country.

2 There has now been a coup d'état in Utopia. The old liberal regime has collapsed and been replaced by a hard-line law and order government. Draft a new set of harsh laws. Report your laws to the other groups and give reasons for the changes you have made.

3 In pairs, discuss the changes that have taken place in Utopia. How have you personally been affected and how do you feel?

# 23 Geography

Describing the people of different countries
Describing the fauna and flora of Britain and your own country

## 23.1 Nationalities

Fill in the gaps:

John comes from England.
He's an Englishman.
He has a British passport.
The English speak English.

Paddy comes from Ireland.
He's an …
He has an … passport.
The … speak English.

Jock comes from Scotland.
He's a …
He has a British passport.
The … speak English, but some also speak …

Taffy comes from Wales.
He's a …
He has a British passport.
The … speak English, but many also speak …

Follow the same pattern to talk about yourself and the others in the class.

## 23.2 'Trafalgar Square'

Imagine you are standing in Trafalgar Square, watching the traffic. You see a lot of foreign cars go past. Talk about each one like this:

A: Oh look! That car comes from *Austria*, doesn't it?
B: That's right: the driver's probably *an Austrian* with *an Austrian* passport.
A: The *Austrians* speak German, don't they?
B: Yes and the capital city is Vienna.
A: Vienna – I see.

Here are some more international plates:

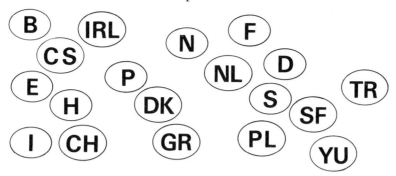

## 23.3 International airlines

Can you say where each of these airlines fly from:

In pairs, imagine you are at a travel agent's inquiring about flights. Follow this pattern conversation:

A: I'd like to fly to *Algeria*. (*Country*)
B: Well, why not go by *Air Algerie*? (*Airline*)
A: Is that *an Algerian* airline? (*Nationality*)
B: Oh yes: all the crew are *Algerians*, they serve delicious *Algerian* food and they all speak *Arabic*, *French* and *English*. (*People, nationality, languages*)
A: Fine! Can you book me a first-class return to *Algiers*, then, please? (*Airport*)
B: Certainly! What date?

79

### 23.4 People, customs, languages

Think of the countries that surround *your* country. Talk about the people, their customs and their languages.

Think of the countries you have visited in your life. Which are the most friendly people? Which is the most tasty food? Which is the most difficult language?

### 23.5 National stereotypes

In groups, find suitable adjectives to describe your personal stereotype of a 'typical' citizen of the following countries. For example:
USA – flamboyant? generous? outspoken?

| | |
|---|---|
| England | Scotland |
| Mexico | Ireland |
| Brazil | Soviet Union |
| France | Germany |
| Italy | Sweden |
| Spain | Your own country |

Discuss the validity of such stereotypes. How true are they?

### 23.6 Wildlife and trees

Imagine you are walking in the British countryside. What can you see around you? In pairs, add four more items to these lists of British fauna and flora:

| | | | |
|---|---|---|---|
| rabbit | sparrow | bee | oak |
| fox | robin | wasp | pine |
| deer | blackbird | grasshopper | chestnut |

Compare your lists with the other groups and describe the ones they don't understand.

Pattern conversation: 'A walk in the country'

A: Look over there! Can you see that *squirrel*!
B: A *squirrel*? You don't see many of those round here.
A: Oh no, it's only a *rabbit*, sorry!
B: They're quite common.
*or* They're quite rare, too.

Follow the pattern, introducing animals and so on from the lists.


## 23.7 Your own country's fauna and flora

Tell everyone else what animals, birds and trees they might see in your country. How is the countryside different from Britain? Do people go for country walks very much?

## 24 Articles

Using definite and zero articles accurately

### 24.1 'A world tour': game to test the use of 'the'

|  |  | *Example* | *Category* |
|---|---|---|---|
| *Round 1* | Last year I sailed to ... | Europe | *continent* |
|  | on ... | the Queen Elizabeth | *name of ship* |
|  | across ... | the Atlantic | *name of sea* |
|  | I then travelled to ... | Switzerland | *country* |
|  | because I wanted to see ... | Lake Geneva | *lake* |
|  | During my stay I crossed ... | the Rhine | *river* |
|  | went up into ... | the Alps | *mountain range* |
|  | And climbed to the top of ... | Mont Blanc | *mountain* |
| *Round 2* | While I was in ... | London | *city* |
|  | I stayed at ... | the Dorchester | *name of hotel* |
|  | visited ... | the National Gallery | *museum* |
|  | and went to ... | the Aldwych | *theatre* |
|  | Every day I read ... | *The Times* | *newspaper* |
|  | and every week I read ... | *Punch* | *magazine* |

Follow the same patterns once for each continent.
Cover up the *example* column.

Follow the patterns twice more for your own continent.
Cover up both right-hand columns.

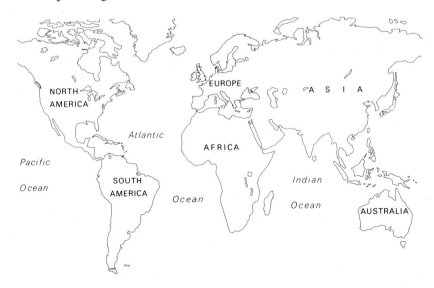

## 24.2 Abstract nouns

A: Do you know much about *science*?
B: Yes, I've been studying *science* for three years.
A: You'll soon be a qualified *scientist*, then.
B: Yes, if I pass the exams!

*In pairs*  Follow the pattern, using these ideas:

| | | |
|---|---|---|
| medicine | physics | nature |
| art | chemistry | commerce |
| education | pharmacy | driving |
| mathematics | history | law |

Later, talk about your *real* knowledge of the subjects and other subjects you have studied.


## 24.3 Mass nouns

A: Did you *hear* the *news*?
B: My goodness yes, what *terrible news*!
A: Oh, I thought it was quite *good news*, myself.
B: Really?

*In pairs*  Follow the pattern, using these variants. You'll need to think of your own opposites for line 3 most of the time!

| | |
|---|---|
| receive – advice – useless | eat – food – tasteless |
| see – furniture – dreadful | do – homework – difficult |
| see – traffic – heavy | hear – applause – unenthusiastic |
| see – accommodation – uncomfortable | notice – his behaviour – rude |
| get – information – boring | read – poetry – dull |

Talk about your own experience and opinions on the topics.


## 24.4 'Institutions'

A: Johnny has to go *to school because he's only 10*.
B: Can I go *to the school* to visit him?
A: No, they don't allow visitors *in the classroom*.
B: What a shame!

*In pairs*  Follow the pattern, using these variants. Make up your own reasons:

court – courtroom
hospital – ward
university – lecture hall
college – library
prison – cell

Talk about your own visits to the places mentioned.

## 25  Holidays

Describing your own experiences of holidays and holiday travel
Stating your preferences in holidays
Talking about tourism

### 25.1  Questionnaire: ask five people

SURVEY ON HOLIDAYS

1. Was your last holiday a package holiday? What made you make this choice?
2. Where did you go and what did you do there?
3. Why did you decide to go there? Would you go there again?
4. What was the best thing about your holiday?
5. What was the worst thing?
6. Where do you dream of going to? Why?
7. Do you like flying? Why (not)?

Report your findings to the class.
What are your own answers to the questions?

### 25.2  Can you use these words?

| | | | |
|---|---|---|---|
| tourist | charter flight | all-in cost | sightseeing |
| holiday-maker | scheduled flight | full board | sunbathing |
| guide | coach tour | half board | winter sports |
| courier | | bed and breakfast | water sports |
| hotelier | | | walking |
| sightseer | | | mountaineering |

Talk about your own last holiday using the words.

### 25.3  What shall we do?

Mountains    Forest    Country    City    Sea-side

A: Let's go to the mountains this summer!
B: What for?
A: We can spend our time mountaineering and enjoying the fresh mountain air and ...
B: That sounds a great idea!

*In pairs*  Follow the pattern to talk about other regions in the diagram. Suggest at least three activities for each region.

## 25.4 Come to ...!

Write notes (or a full account) of the attractions of a resort in your country. Then make a short speech to the others about it.

## 25.5 The ski-ing resort

The mountain village of Bergdorf has for a long time been off the beaten track and only visited by a few tourists in the summer. Now a consortium of businessmen from a town in the valley have come up with a plan for the village to be developed into a ski-resort. A tourist complex of hotels, apartments, boutiques, a swimming pool and other luxury facilities would be built to attract winter-sports enthusiasts. A public meeting to discuss the plans will take place tomorrow. Meanwhile, the pros and cons of the plan are being discussed in the village inn, mayor's office and private houses.

*Choose your role:*

Mayor of the village: supports the scheme
Chairman of development consortium
Innkeeper: could expand his business
Shopkeeper: could make a lot of money selling equipment
Famous writer: lives in village but not a native – enjoys rural peace
Weekend resident: works in town, gets away from it all in his weekend cottage
Journalist: sent from town to report on the meeting
Old man: doesn't like change
Old woman: may not live to see benefits of scheme
Young person: unemployed
Doctor: thinks scheme would destroy village life
Schoolboy: no prospects for work
Schoolgirl: finds village 'dead'
Farmer: does not like tourists
Farmer's wife: difficult to make ends meet
Nature Reserve warden: scheme would destroy wild life

Outline the standpoint and character of your chosen role.

Study the development plan on the next page.

The scheme will take 5 years to complete.
When construction is finished there will be:

400 hotel beds
150 private apartments
15 shops and boutiques
1 supermarket
1 bank
7 ski-lifts with access to 150 km of ski-runs
Improved road and rail access to the valley

THE COMPLETED SCHEME                    THE VILLAGE TODAY

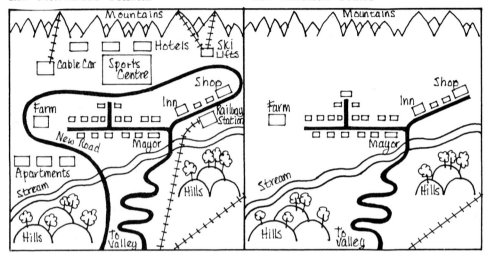

1 Divide the classroom into four areas: inn, mayor's office, shop, farmhouse. Visit each place and discuss the scheme there for a few minutes, before moving on.

### Useful language

How do you feel about …?
I don't like the idea of …
I'm in two minds about …
I'm all in favour of …
There are an enormous number of advantages/disadvantages in …

2 Move the classroom chairs to represent rows of chairs (for the public) and a platform (for the mayor and the chairman of the consortium). First the chairman is introduced by the mayor and answers questions from the public. Then the public present their views for or against the scheme. Finally, a vote is taken.

3 Divide the room into the same four areas and discuss the outcome of the meeting with the others there.

# 26 Reporting

Reporting conversations using appropriate reporting verbs
Reporting tones of voice

## 26.1 The time factor

Colin rings up Alan and asks about Bob:

C: Is Bob feeling better?
A: (*at the time*) Colin wants to know if you're feeling better.
A: (*a few minutes later*) Colin wanted to know if you're feeling better.
A: (*next day or even later*) Colin wanted to know if you were feeling better.

Discuss with your teacher the reasons for the changes of tense.

Look at this telephone conversation:

'Hallo, Alan ... This is Colin speaking ... fine! How about you? ... Good, and how's Bob feeling after his holiday? ... I see. I've got quite a lot to tell you. I've just got engaged ... Yes ... No, we haven't fixed a date yet ... What's she like? Lovely girl – we met on a bus, believe it or not ... Yes, we just happened to be sitting together and got into conversation. Then we made a date for the same evening and discovered we'd got a lot in common – you know, same interests and we laugh at the same things ... No, you don't know her – at least she doesn't know you or Bob ... Oh about three weeks now ... Well, yes it was quite a sudden decision but I feel really happy ... I'd like you both to meet her, how about a meal together one evening soon. Could you ask Bob to ring me. Must go now, my boss has just come into the office ... Bye ... Oh, thanks ... Bye.'

Fill in the gaps with Alan's words.

Imagine first that Alan has answered the phone because Bob is at the other end of the office and can't come to the phone. Report the conversation to Bob using:

He wants to know ... (+ *same tense as the conversation*)
He says ...
He wants you/us to ...

Now imagine that Alan has answered the phone because Bob is out of the office. Report the conversation to Bob when he returns ten minutes later. Use:

He wanted to know ... (+ *same tense as the conversation*)
He said ...
He wants you/us to ...

Finally, imagine that Alan answered the phone while Bob was on a business trip to Canada. A week later Colin broke off the engagement. Report the original conversation to Bob on his return using:

He wanted to know ... (+ *verb put back into past*)
He said ...
He wanted you/us to ...


## 26.2    More telephone conversations

*In threes*    Take it in turns to improvise several more conversations like the one given in 26.1. Invent your own news and information. When you play the part of A (the receiver of the call) you may well need to make notes. Decide whether B is to *either* be present during the call *or* to come back soon after the call *or* to come back 'the next day'.


## 26.3    Reporting ways of influencing people

Can you use these words?

I ordered him to ...
I told him to ...
I got him to ...
I urged him to ...
I begged him to ...
I reminded him to ...
I persuaded him to ...
I advised him to ...
I recommended him to ...
I encouraged him to ...
I asked him to ...
I warned him to ...
I invited him to ...

I insisted that he ...
I suggested that he ...
I recommended that he ...

I promised that I ...
I threatened that I ...

I offered to ...
I promised to ...
I threatened to ...

In threes or pairs, imagine *one* possible situation when these remarks might be made. Then decide on the most appropriate way to report them:

Stand up straight!
Can you lend me 2p?

You must be more careful next time.
If you don't tell me, I'll be very cross.

Oh, please let me go – please!
You'd better go to bed.
Feel like coming round tonight?
The best thing to do is spend it.

I'd say you should at least try to do it.
Tomorrow, 6 o'clock! Alright?
You have no choice, you've got to answer.
I'll help you if you ask me.

Compare your situations and reports with the other groups.

## 26.4 Reporting statements, questions and responses

Can you use these words?

| He | stated | that … (*statement*) |
| | announced | |
| | told her | |
| | informed her | |
| | declared | |
| | remarked | |
| | reported | |
| | emphasized | |

| She | inquired | whether … (*question*) |
| | wondered | |
| | wanted to know | |
| | asked him | |

| He | replied | that … (*response*) |
| | answered | |
| | said | |
| | told her | |
| | informed her | |
| | confessed | |
| | admitted | |
| | agreed | |
| | protested | |
| | denied | |

In threes or pairs, decide on a likely situation each of these conversations might occur in. Then work out how you would report them.

He: I heard on the news that there's been another demonstration.
She: Where was this one?
He: Outside a language school this time.

He: It is very important to remember that the law must be changed.
She: Didn't you say the other day it was a fair law?
He: Well, yes I may well have done … but I've changed my mind.

He: It's raining again, I see.
She: Does it look as if it'll stop soon?
He: Not really.

He: I've passed my exam!
She: Congratulations! What are your plans now?
He: I might decide to go to college after all.

89

He: There's a lot of work to do.
She: No, there isn't!
He: Isn't there? No, you're right.

Compare your situations and reports with the other groups.

## 26.5 Reporting tones of voice

Can you use these words?

| | |
|---|---|
| shout | swear |
| whisper | mutter |
| stutter | sneer |
| stammer | grumble |
| exclaim | scream |

Try 'acting' each of the sentences below in several different tones of voice. Get the others to respond, using an appropriate verb. For example:

A: (*shouting*) What dreadful weather!!
B: There's no need to shout!
C: Please don't shout so loudly!

What dreadful weather!
What time is it?
I feel a bit sick.

# 27  Education

Describing your own school career
Talking about education systems and educational methods

## 27.1  Education systems: simplified description

*England and Wales*                    *Your country*

```
Age   1
      2
      3     Pre-school (play groups)
      4
      5     Primary School or First School
      6
      7
      8
      9                      Middle School
     10
     11     Comprehensive School
     12
     13                      Comprehensive School
     14
     15
     16
     17
     18     University or College or Polytechnic
     19
     20
     21         3 or 4 year course
     22
     23     Post-graduate studies
     24
     25
```

Compulsory schooling

Sixth-form College

Describe the English system.
Draw a similar chart for your own country and describe the differences.

## 27.2  School subjects

*In groups*  Tick off on this list the subjects you studied at school:

| | | |
|---|---|---|
| Maths | Geography | English |
| Physics | Home economics | Another foreign language |
| Chemistry | Handicrafts | Your own language and literature |
| Botany | Religion | Economics |
| Zoology | Sport | Politics |
| History | Art (painting) | Typing |

Did you study any other subjects not included in the list?

91

Answer these questions:

1  Which were you best at?
2  Which did you enjoy most? Why?
3  Which are you still studying or interested in?
4  Which are still relevant to your life? How?
5  Which do you regret not studying? Why?

Did you enjoy your schooldays? Why (not)?

## 27.3  Abbreviations

Find out what these abbreviations mean:

CSE
GCE O Level and A Level
B.A.
B.Sc.
Cert. Ed.
Dip. Ed.
M.A.
Ph.D.

What equivalent qualifications are there in your country?

## 27.4  Talking points

*In groups*  State and justify your point of view on these controversial aspects of education. What is your own personal experience of them?

Comprehensive Schools or Grammar Schools
Specialization in Secondary School
Private education (and 'Public Schools')
Compulsory schooling from 5 to 16
Single-sex or co-educational schools
School uniforms
Academic or vocational schooling
University grants
Starting University at 18
Pupils controlling school curriculum
Examinations
What is a 'good teacher' and a 'bad teacher'?

Report your discussion on one of the points to the other groups.

## 27.5  Your own schooling

Write an account of your own school career.
Describe your own progress through the system. What subjects did you enjoy and so on (look again at 27.2 for ideas)?

### 27.6  'Educational planning committee'

*In groups*  Your school or college has introduced a new Committee system of planning programmes of studies. This involves co-operation and consultation between:

the Director of Studies
the Head of Department
the teachers
the students

In groups, select your role and decide on a well-balanced, varied and interesting programme for:
a)  your own class
b)  a beginner's class

(It may help to get a selection of text-books and read the 'blurb' on each cover before you begin. Also flip through each book to get an idea of the contents.)

When you have planned your two programmes, report back to the Financial Director (your teacher).

## 28  Degree

Using intensifying and degree adverbs appropriately
Using 'as … as …' and 'like a …' idioms
Describing your reactions

### 28.1  Very

A: What was it like?
B: It was

| | |
|---|---|
| ever so | nice. |
| extremely | pleasant. |
| really | tasty. |
| very very | nasty. |
| really very | unpleasant. |
| awfully | |
| terribly | |
| incredibly | |
| very | |

In pairs, ask each other about these things which you ate recently:

| | |
|---|---|
| scrambled egg | baked potatoes |
| grilled worm | baked beans |
| snake pie | grilled sausages |
| roast beef | home-made cake |
| fried fish | supermarket cake |

Talk about food you have really eaten recently.

### 28.2  Absolutely

A: What was it like?
B: It was

| | |
|---|---|
| absolutely | delicious! |
| really | fantastic! |
| | superb! |
| | amazing! |
| | marvellous! |

*or* It was

| | |
|---|---|
| absolutely | disgusting! |
| really | terrible! |
| | awful! |
| | appalling! |
| | dreadful! |

In pairs, ask each other about these things which you drank recently:

freshly-pressed orange juice      espresso coffee
sea water      sour milk
cold soup      vintage Burgundy
flat orangeade      cough medicine

Talk about real drinks you have had recently.

!★CAREFUL★! If you are talking to someone who has given you unpleasant food or drink it is more polite to say:

'It's not quite what I'm used to.'
*or* 'It's not quite to my taste.'

## 28.3 Pretty

A: What was it like?

| B: It was | pretty | good. |
|---|---|---|
|  | fairly | nice. |
|  | quite |  |
|  | reasonably |  |

| *or* It was | pretty | bad. |
|---|---|---|
|  | rather | nasty. |
|  | somewhat |  |

In pairs, follow the pattern using these prompts:

film – exciting      evening – dull
book – difficult      meal – rich
match – entertaining      writing – unclear
cigar – strong      exam – easy

## 28.4 Books and films

*In groups*      Think of two books – one you enjoyed and one you hated. And two films. Describe your reactions to the others and *give reasons*.

## 28.5 As easy as winking: some useful idioms

Fill in the gaps first.

When would you use these expressions to describe people?

| As | drunk | as a | lord |
|---|---|---|---|
|  | sober |  | judge |
|  | quiet |  | mouse |
|  |  |  | fox |
|  |  |  | sheet |
|  |  |  | fiddle |
|  |  |  | picture |

| As | | | flash |
|---|---|---|---|
| | | | daisy |
| | | | church mouse |
| | | | feather |
| | | | hatter |
| | | | peacock |
| | | | post |
| | sick | | dog |

| As | good | as | gold |
|---|---|---|---|
| | | | sin |
| | | | two short planks |
| | regular | | clockwork |
| | cold | | ice |

Cover up the right-hand column of each list and *remember* the expressions.
In pairs, test each other.

Find another way of expressing each idea in the list, using the intensifiers introduced in 28.1 and 28.2. For example:
'He was as drunk as a lord.' – 'He was awfully drunk.'


## 28.6 'Like a . . .' idioms

When would you use these expressions?

| He | drinks | like a | fish. |
|---|---|---|---|
| | eats | | pig. |
| | eats | | horse. |
| | drives | | lunatic. |
| | smokes | | chimney. |
| | swears | | trooper. |
| | slept | | log. |

Cover up the list and *remember* the idioms. Test each other.


## 28.7 Storytime

Tell a story round the class, beginning 'Once upon a time ...'. Each narrator must use *one* idiom from 28.5 or 28.6 before he can pass the narrative on to the next student.

## 29 Isn't it?

Using negative questions, echo questions and tags appropriately and accurately

### 29.1 Surprised responses: negative questions

 A: It was quite warm yesterday, I seem to remember.
B: Oh, wasn't it *cold*? ↑ (*Rising tone*)
A: No, I'm quite sure it was warm.
B: *Oh.* ↓ (*Falling tone*)

Practise the intonation. What does 'Oh' mean here?

In pairs, follow the same pattern and make surprised responses. Respond with the *opposite* of these opening remarks:

| | |
|---|---|
| It was hot. | He's become rich. |
| She's stupid. | They've been good. |
| They've been ill. | He spoke politely. |
| He arrived early. | She was beautiful. |
| They were noisy. | It tasted sweet. |
| He likes tall girls. | |

!★CAREFUL★! about the intonation.

### 29.2 Expressing disbelief: echo questions

 A: I think it's quite difficult.
B: It's quite *difficult*? ↑
   That's funny, I thought it was *easy*. ↓
A: No, I'm sure it's difficult.
B: *Oh?* ↑

Practise the intonation. What does 'Oh' mean here?

In pairs, follow the same pattern and respond to these opening remarks:

| | |
|---|---|
| It rained yesterday. | He likes pop music. |
| There were very few people at the lecture. | They drive on the left in Canada. |
| I can't swim. | She was polite. |
| It's an interesting book. | They looked sad. |
| It was a complicated story. | |

!★CAREFUL★! about the verb forms.

## 29.3 Contradicting mildly: tag questions

A: John says the weather was good.
B: No, it was *bad*, wasn't it? ↑
A: I don't know – that's what he says.
B: Well, as far as I know, it was *bad*. ↓
A: I see.

Practise the intonation.

In pairs, follow the same pattern with these opening remarks:

| John | says | the exam is difficult. |
| Rob | tells me | most candidates fail. |
| Sue | | everyone passed last year. |
| Michael | | we've got no chance of getting through. |
| Belinda | | there are very few lucky candidates. |
| Jan | | John's fat. |
| Adrian | | Mary used to be shy. |
| Alan | | John was a beautiful baby. |
| Perry | | Mary likes talkative people. |
| Richard | | John and Mary drink a lot of coffee. |

## 29.4 'The United Kingdom'

*In groups*    Here are some true and false facts about Britain – only one fact in each line is true. First decide which facts you personally think are the true ones. In each group of three or four, one person begins with a fact and the others react with surprise, with disbelief, or contradict mildly – as practised in 29.1–29.3.

| THE UNITED KINGDOM | | | | |
|---|---|---|---|---|
| Population | 36M | 46M | 56M | 66M |
| Area | 140,000 sq km | 240,000 sq km | 340,000 sq km | 440 sq km |
| Cities over 500,000 | 7 | 8 | 9 | 10 |
| Second city | Manchester | Birmingham | Glasgow | Liverpool |
| Compulsory school age | 4-15 | 5-15 | 5-16 | 6-16 |
| Warmest month | May | June | July | August |
| Coldest month | December | January | February | March |
| Wettest month | November | January | February | April |
| MPs | 335 | 435 | 535 | 635 |
| Motorways | 500 km | 1000 km | 1500 km | 2000 km |

Find out what is true if you are still not sure after the discussion.

### 29.5 'Clever dick'

*In pairs*  A 'clever dick' is someone who knows everything – or *thinks* he does! Divide into clever dicks and 'normal' people. The clever dick makes a series of untrue statements to which his partner reacts. Here are a few ideas to begin with:

Today is Sunday.
Tomorrow is …
The time is …
Travel by air is …
Supermarkets are …

Change roles half-way.

### 29.6 Getting your listener's agreement: tag questions

 A: English can be called a world language, *can't* it? ↓
B: That's right.
It certainly can.

We can perform the same function by saying:

Don't you *agree* that … ↓
*or* You know …, *don't* you? ↓

Here are some more assertions you want your listener to agree with.
Do the practice in pairs.

Homework is important.
It can help you to remember what you learn.
It fixes what you learn in your long-term memory.
It's no good learning if you forget quickly.
But you also have to speak English outside school.

These things are obvious really.
Life was better in the good old days.
People talked to each other more.
Soon we'll forget the art of conversation.
Television has ruined family life.
People don't care about each other any more.
It's difficult to disagree with me.

*! CAREFUL !* Use the falling tone ↓ .

### 29.7 Free practice

*In pairs*  Choose a subject you feel strongly about or know a lot about and try to impose your views on your partner. If you use a lot of tag questions like the ones in 29.6 it's quite difficult for your listener to contradict you.

### 29.8 Paying compliments: negative question form

 A: Do you like my new shoes?
B: Oh yes, aren't they *smart*! ↓
A: Thank you.

In pairs, fish for compliments on all the clothes you're wearing.

In pairs, fish for more compliments on your:

handwriting
English pronunciation
spoken English
homework
car
house
the view from your room

# 30  Food

Describing methods of preparing and cooking food
Being a customer in a restaurant
Talking about what dishes you like and dislike
Talking about eating habits in Britain and your own country

## 30.1  Home cooking: essential language

Add more words to each of these lists:

| Utensils and gadgets | | | Preparation | |
|---|---|---|---|---|
| frying pan | | | peel | teaspoonful |
| saucepan | | | slice | |
| **Ingredients** | | | **Cooking** | |
| beef | flour | carrots | apples | boil | raw |
| pork | salt | cucumber | pears | fry | over-cooked |

Test each other by asking questions like: 'What do you call that thing you ...?' or 'What do you call it when you ...?'. Or by miming.

## 30.2  Cooking your favourite dish

Describe in detail the ingredients you need and the method of preparation and cooking. While you are listening to someone else speaking, show your reactions appropriately.

### Useful language

Mmm!
That sounds delicious!
That'd taste superb!
I expect that'd look really tasty!
*or*
Ugh!
That sounds disgusting!
I'm not sure I'd like that.

### 30.3 Eating out: essential language

Can you use these words and phrases?

| | |
|---|---|
| menu | starter |
| set meal (table d'hôte) | main course |
| à la carte meal | dessert |
| wine list | chef |

 Waiter!
Miss!
I'd like … to start with and … to follow.
Is … served with …?
What would you recommend?
What is … exactly?
Have you got any … this evening?

### 30.4 In a restaurant

*Improvisation in groups*

In this improvisation each group should represent a different country. You are the proprietors of a restaurant specializing in the cuisine of that country. Work out an ideal menu which gives customers plenty of choice and variety. Write the menu out neatly on a menu card.

Each restaurant should have a table for its customers. Leaving behind two waiters/waitresses, the others in the group should visit the other restaurants and order a meal. After the meal they go back to work as waiters/waitresses and so on.

Discuss the improvisation between turns and afterwards.

### 30.5 Some corny restaurant jokes

Waiter, there's a fly in my soup!
Shh! Don't talk too loud – everyone will want one.

Waiter, there's a fly in my soup!
There's a spider on the bread, he'll catch it.

What's this fly doing in my soup?
I think it's doing the back-stroke, sir.

There's a dead fly swimming in my soup!
That's impossible, a dead fly can't swim.

There's a dead fly in my soup!
Yes sir, it's the hot liquid that kills them.

Waiter, there's a fly in my soup!
Yes sir – we give extra meat rations on Fridays.

Waiter, there's a fly in my soup!
Don't worry sir, there's no extra charge.

## 30.6   Eating habits

Here are some typical British 'family menus':

| | |
|---|---|
| **TRADITIONAL BREAKFAST**<br><br>Porridge<br>Fried eggs and bacon<br>Toast and marmalade | **LIGHT BREAKFAST**<br><br>Cereal<br>Toast and marmalade<br>Coffee |
| **SUNDAY LUNCH**<br><br>Roast pork with apple sauce<br>Roast potatoes<br>Brussels sprouts<br>*<br>Blackberry and apple crumble<br>and custard<br>*<br>White wine | **PUB LUNCH**<br><br>Ploughman's Lunch (bread and cheese)<br>with pickled onions<br>Pint of bitter |
| | **DINNER OUT**<br><br>Prawn cocktail<br>Steak with chips and vegetables<br>Cheese and biscuits<br>Red wine |
| **CREAM TEA**<br><br>Scones with clotted cream<br>and jam<br>Fruit cake<br>Tea | **SUPPER SNACK**<br><br>Baked beans on toast<br>Tea |

Compare these menus with your own experience of British families. And with family food in your own country.

## 30.7   British food

 Look at these comments made by visitors to Britain:

'They overcook their vegetables.'
'They overcook their steaks.'
'They don't use enough herbs.'
'They have potatoes and peas with everything.'
'They eat too much tinned and frozen food.'
'They don't eat enough fresh fruit.'

Most British people would be upset or annoyed if you made these comments to their faces.

It's better to be more *tactful*, like this:

'In my country, we tend to prefer our vegetables cooked a little less than the British.'

Express the other comments in a similarly tactful way. Make up two more comments from your own experience of British food. What critical comments do visitors make on *your* country's food?

**30.8   Questionnaire: ask five people**

Ask five people outside the class to answer these questions:

SURVEY ON FOOD AND HEALTH

1. Do you watch your weight?
2. Have you ever been on a diet?  Why?
3. Do you buy brown bread, wholemeal flour and other health foods?
4. Do you avoid eating butter, cream and cheese?
5. What do you think of vegetarianism?
6. Do you eat three full meals a day?
7. How often do you eat out?
8. What sort of foreign food do you like?

Report your findings to the class and discuss them.
What are your own answers to the questions?

# 31 Gerunds and infinitives

Talking accurately about likes and dislikes, advisability, remembering and trying
Using verbs followed by gerund or infinitive accurately

## 31.1 Liking and disliking

| Mmm! | I enjoy ... | + -ing | Ugh! | I hate ... | + -ing |
|---|---|---|---|---|---|
| | I quite like ... | | | I don't enjoy ... | |
| | I love ... | | | I dislike ... | |
| | I adore ... | | | I loathe ... | |
| | I'm keen on ... | | | I detest ... | |
| | I'm fond of ... | | | I'm not keen on ... | |
| | | | | I can't stand ... | |
| | | | | I can't bear ... | |

I'd like to ...    + infinitive
I'd love to ...
I'm keen to ...
I want to ...
I feel like ...    + -ing

I'd hate to ...    + infinitive
I wouldn't like to ...
I don't want to ...
I don't fancy ...    + -ing
I don't feel like ...    + -ing

How do you feel about these things?

| cowboy films | German films | oysters | peas |
| horror films | Japanese films | tripe | gravy |
| Hollywood epics | detective films | steak | custard |
| science fiction films | documentary films | snails | apple pie |
| sex films | romantic films | mashed potatoes | roast beef |

And how much would you like to see or eat them this evening?

Make a list of your five favourite composers or musicians or your five favourite painters.
Say why you like them and get the others to say how they feel about them.

## 31.2   Is it a good idea?

Useful language

It's not worth ...          + -ing          It's well worth ...     + -ing
There's no point in ...                      It's a good idea to ... + infinitive
It's no good ...                             It's best to ...        + infinitive
It's no use ...
It's useless ...
It's a waste of | time ...
                | money ...
                | effort ...
                | energy ...
It's futile ...
It's better not to ...      + infinitive
You'd better not ...        + infinitive
It's not a good idea to ... + infinitive

Answer these questions, using the expressions above:

a)  If there's a long queue outside a cinema, is it worth joining the queue?
b)  If you want to improve your English, is it worth spending a year in the USA?
c)  If you live in a safe Conservative seat, is it worth voting Labour?

In groups, discuss the advisability of doing these things and the *methods* you might use to do them:

Making your own | bread
                | beer
                | wine
                | clothes

Repairing your own | car
                   | watch
                   | hi-fi
                   | telephone

## 31.3   Remember

B has just returned from town in the evening –
A had asked her in the morning to do some shopping, and even reminded her at lunchtime:

A: Did you remember to get the bread?
B: Well, I remember walking past the baker's shop ...
A: But you forgot to get the bread?
B: I'm afraid so. I don't remember you telling me to get it.
A: Well, I certainly did. In fact I reminded you to get it at lunchtime.

Here is the shopping list B didn't take. Act out the pattern conversation in pairs, changing roles half-way:

# Shopping List

Bread      Sun oil

Fish    wine    tickets

Carrots      evening paper

dog food      matches   LP

MONEY !

What things did you forget to buy last time you went shopping?
What shops do you remember going into the last time you went to town?

## 31.4   Try

A: So the door was closed?
B: Yes, I tried to open it by turning the handle, but that didn't work. So I tried shaking it and I tried pushing it. It still wouldn't open, so then I tried kicking it and at last I succeeded in opening it.

Follow the pattern to answer these questions – you'll need to invent three unsuccessful attempts and a successful one for each problem:

So your car wouldn't start?
So the dog started to attack you?
So the boat started to sink?
So a fire broke out?
So the baby started crying?

What should you try to do and try doing if you:

smoke too much
don't want to forget your English
are too fat
are lonely
want people to like you

### 31.5 More verbs: A–L

Use your own ideas to complete these sentences:

| | | |
|---|---|---|
| I can't afford | to | |
| In an exam you aren't allowed | to | |
| A dog was sitting in the road but he avoided | | -ing |
| Very carefully he began | to | |
| No employer would ever consider | | -ing |
| I have now decided | to | |
| He's still here – he's delayed | | -ing |
| If you don't work hard you deserve | to | |
| The money was lost – I failed | to | |
| Please finish | | -ing |
| The secret police forced him | to | |
| I've decided to give up | | -ing |
| Please help me | to | |
| I'm afraid I can't help | | -ing |
| It's annoying if you keep (on) | | -ing |
| Will you please let me | | |
| After three months away from home I'm longing | to | |
| I'm really looking forward to | | -ing |

1 Cover up the centre column and remember.
2 Cover up the last two columns and remember.


### 31.6 More verbs: M–V

Use your own ideas to complete these sentences:

| | | |
|---|---|---|
| I didn't want to do it – they made me | | |
| Would you mind | | -ing |
| In the winter I really miss | | -ing |
| I'm sorry I didn't notice you | | -ing |
| I can't permit you | to | |
| We can't permit | | -ing |
| Because of the rain we postponed | | -ing |
| The fisherman prepared | to | |
| If you're bored you must pretend | to | |
| Yes, I promise | to | |
| In a shop I resent | | -ing |
| You'll just have to risk | | -ing |
| He spent twenty minutes | | -ing |
| It's time to start | | -ing |
| If your car won't start I suggest | | -ing |
| When I was young I used | to | |
| I'm not used to | | -ing |
| I want someone to volunteer | to | |

1 Cover up the centre column and remember.
2 Cover up the last two columns and remember.

## 31.7  Consequences

Each player needs a long strip of paper, half an A4 sheet is ideal. He writes one line of the story (a complete sentence) and folds the paper so that the writing is not visible and hands it on to the next player to write the second line. At the end everyone opens up his paper and reads out what is written.

1. *Name of person in class*
2. Because...
3. And also...
4. However...
5. So...
6. But...
7. So everybody...

Choose one of these words to use in each line. Remember to write a complete sentence each time!

| | |
|---|---|
| looking forward | try |
| keen | remember |
| no point | not worth |
| used to | let |
| remind | fond |
| enjoy | feel like |

# 32  Politics

Stating your political beliefs
Describing the political system in your country

## 32.1  Can you use these words?

| Ultraleft | Marxist | Left-wing | Socialist | Middle of the road | Conservative | Right-wing | Fascist | Ultraright |
|---|---|---|---|---|---|---|---|---|
| | Progressive | | | Centre | | Reactionary | | |

We believe in ...                    We don't believe in ...
We're in favour of ...               We're against ...
We support ...                       We reject ...
We approve of ...                    We disapprove of ...
We're campaigning for ...            We're campaigning against ...

candidate          constituency
MP                 vote
                   election

Discuss *when* you would use each expression.

## 32.2  Politics in your country

Describe the political system in your country. How is the country governed and what political parties are there?
Which way is your country likely to turn at the next election?

## 32.3  Political issues: talking points

*In groups*  What are your own views on these political issues?
What is the attitude of most of your fellow-countrymen?

Nationalization                              The power of the trade unions
Defence spending                             The freedom of the press
Devolution of power (regional government)    Distribution of wealth
Taxation

Report your discussion to the other groups.

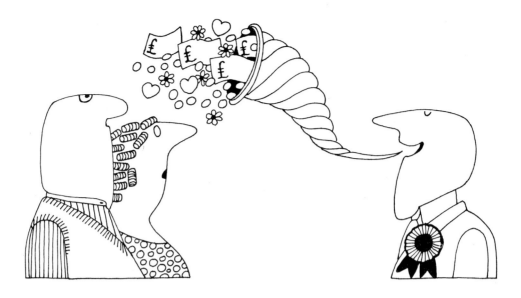

## 32.4    A general election

*In groups*    You are in the country of Teflonia where there are two political parties. Here are their policies:

| Royalist Party Manifesto | Republican Party Manifesto |
|---|---|
| 1. Increase the power of the monarch. | 1. Abolish the monarchy. |
| 2. Remove tax on wines and spirits. | 2. Higher taxes on wines and spirits. |
| 3. Stop sales of cigarettes. | 3. Make cigarettes cheaper. |
| 4. Introduce tax on all children. | 4. Parents of two or more children need pay no tax. |
| 5. Cut defence spending. | 5. Increase military forces. |
| 6. Introduce means test for education. | 6. Improve educational system. |
| 7. De-nationalize railways, post office, power supply. | 7. Nationalize all retail shops and oil companies. |
| 8. | 8. |
| 9. | 9. |

1 Split up into two groups. Royalists and Republicans.
   Add two more policies to your manifesto. Then choose a parliamentary candidate.

2 Now you are a paid-up member of one of the parties, canvas some people from the other party and argue your case with them.

3 The two candidates should now make a short eve-of-election speech. Heckling may take place and questions may be asked. Then hold the election. The king or queen (teacher) will count the votes.

4 Now the results are out there has been a call for a coalition government. What policies of each party are to be retained and why?

## 33   Sequence of events

Describing and discussing the sequence of events and activities
Joining sentences with time expressions

### 33.1   Introduction: sentence-joining

'I finished the meal *and* did the washing-up.'

There are four more important ways of joining sentences:

a)  Using an -ing form:

'Having finished the meal, I did the washing-up.'
'After finishing the meal, I did the washing-up.'
(These are mostly used in formal written style.)

b)  Using a preposition:

'After the meal I did the washing-up.'

c)  Using a conjunction:

'Once I had finished the meal, I did the washing-up.'
'After I had finished the meal, I did the washing-up.'
'As soon as I had finished the meal, I did the washing-up.'
'When I (had) finished the meal, I did the washing-up.'

d)  Using linking adverbs to join sentences across a full-stop:

'I finished the meal. Then I did the washing-up.'
'I finished the meal. Afterwards I did the washing-up.'

When would you use these methods of joining sentences?

Use *before* and *beforehand* to join the same sentences.

### 33.2   A tour of Europe: before you go

You are about to set off on a motoring tour of Europe. Opposite is a map of your planned itinerary:

Things to do and get *before* you set off:

| | | |
|---|---|---|
| travellers cheques | cancel papers | guidebook |
| renew passport | lock back door | maps |
| book ferry tickets | | pack |
| have car serviced | | |

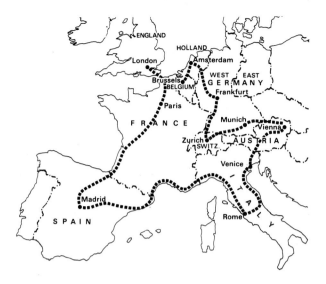

In groups, talk about what you have to do before you set off.
Use structures like these:

A: I've got to get some travellers cheques before I set off.
B: After I've got some travellers cheques, I'll be ready to leave.
C: I must get some travellers cheques. Then I'll be ready to go.
D: Don't forget to get some travellers cheques. Then you'll be ready to set off.
E: Before you go, remember to get some travellers cheques.

Each member of the group should give the same information in a different way.


## 33.3  Planning

*In groups*  You have one day to spend in each city on your journey.
Plan what you're going to do and see in each. Decide what you're going to do first. Like this:

Paris: go up Eiffel Tower        2
       take trip on the Seine    1
       go round the Louvre       3
       visit Crazy Horse Saloon  4

'I'd like to take a trip on the Seine before I go up the Eiffel Tower.'
'Let's go round the Louvre. Afterwards we can go to the Crazy Horse Saloon.'
and so on with your plans for these cities:

| | | | | |
|---|---|---|---|---|
| Madrid | Venice | Munich | Frankfurt | Brussels |
| Rome | Vienna | Zurich | Amsterdam | London |

Discuss your priorities.

### Useful language

Wouldn't it be better to …          Personally, I'd prefer to …
On the other hand we could …        Well, while you're …, I'd prefer to …
Why don't we …

## 33.4 Later...

You're now near the end of your journey, having a chat over a meal in Ostend as you wait for the car ferry. Remember all the things you had to do before setting off:

'We didn't set off until we'd had the car serviced.'
'Before setting off we had the car serviced.'
'We set off on Tuesday. By then we'd had the car serviced.'

*But:*

'The moment we got to Southampton, I couldn't remember if I'd locked the back door.'
'Once I'd phoned Mrs Jones next-door, I felt much better.'

Continue the conversation in groups, referring back to 33.2 if necessary.

Now remember what you did during your holiday. Refer back to 33.3 if necessary.

## 33.5 Write

Describe the most interesting places you visited on the tour and what you saw there.

## 33.6 A seven-day tour of Britain

Plan a tour *before* you come to class, bearing in mind that you want to see as much as possible *and* avoid being on the road all the time.

In groups, discuss your various plans and try to achieve a mutually acceptable compromise. Then explain your plan to the others.

(If you are not at all familiar with Britain, you might prefer to design a tour of your own country. Discuss this possibility with your teacher.)

## 34  Work

Describing your own and other people's work
Talking about careers
Being interviewed

### 34.1  Other people's work

Here are some well-known occupations and professions:

photographer
gardener
singer
lawyer
window-cleaner
interpreter
taxi-driver

burglar
beggar

musician
politician
electrician
librarian
mathematician

sailor
governor
translator
decorator
professor

salesman
cameraman
businessman
milkman
policeman

scientist
chemist
physicist
cartoonist
economist

Describe the work that each of the above people do. For example:

'A gardener works in a garden. He plants seeds, he grows flowers and vegetables, he mows the lawn and he spends a lot of time digging and weeding.'

Describe your own job in the same way.

## 34.2  Places of work

Here are some places of work and fields of interest. Decide which jobs or professions would be involved with each. Then describe the sort of work they might do. For example:

hospital:  'One person who works in a hospital is a surgeon. He performs operations on
people and he works in an operating theatre.'
'Another person who works in a hospital is a nurse. She …'

| | | |
|---|---|---|
| coal mine | forest | meat |
| office | army | bread |
| farm | bank | milk |
| ship | laboratory | fish |
| lorry | studio | rubbish |
| department store | prison | windows |
| pub | zoo | tax |
| restaurant | factory | |
| theatre | railway | |
| opera house | garage | |
| government office | night club | |

With this practice you can go round the class or round the group with each student adding another member of the staff of each place in the list.

## 34.3  Game: 'What's my line?'

Each contestant mimes one activity involved in a well-known (or unusual) job. The others have to guess the name of the job by asking questions. The contestant can only answer 'Yes' or 'No' and he beats the panel if they can't get the answer after ten questions. This game can be played in groups.

## 34.4  Careers: talking points

*In groups*  What do you look for in a job?
Is it a good idea to change jobs frequently?
What do you plan to be doing in two years' time and in ten years' time?
What are the good points and bad points of your present job (or of being a student)?

## 34.5  Questionnaire: ask five people

---
WORK SURVEY

1. What is your job exactly?  What sort of work do you do on a
   typical day?
2. Do you belong to a trade union?  Why (not)?
3. How many hours a day do you work?
4. What do you enjoy most about your job?
5. What do you hate most about your job?

---

Report your findings to the others. What are your reactions to the reports you hear?

### 34.6    A new teacher

*In groups*    Your school or college needs an English teacher.
Write an advertisement for this post.
Decide and make notes of what questions you would ask applicants at an interview.

Each group interviews one applicant (one of the applicants can be your teacher, the others volunteer students). After about ten minutes the applicants change to another interviewing panel and so on. Each group decides on the best applicant and gives reasons for the choice.

### 34.7    Interviews: talking points

What sort of impressions should you try to make at an interview?
What sort of questions should the interviewee ask the interviewer?
Should you ever tell lies or adapt the truth at an interview?
What sort of preparation should the interviewer and interviewee do before they meet?

### 34.8    Difficult questions

Imagine you are being interviewed for a job you really want. How would you answer these questions?

 What was the worst problem you encountered in your present job? How did you handle it?
Why do you want to leave your present job?
What are you most proud of having done in your present job?
Why do you think you are qualified for this job?
What sort of boss would you most like to work for?
Supposing a member of your staff was frequently away from work, claiming to be ill, what action would you take?
If you are working as part of a team, what unspoken rules of behaviour would you observe?
How long do you plan to stay in this job?

In pairs, improvise a job interview where these questions are asked. Ask other awkward questions, too.

#### Useful language

 I'd like to think about that one.
Let me see ...
The best way I can answer that is to say ...

Another 'delaying tactic' is to repeat the question you have been asked, like this:
'How long do I plan to stay, well ...'

# 35 Punctuation!

Punctuating written sentences accurately

## 35.1 Punctuation rules

When would you use these punctuation marks and other devices?

| | |
|---|---|
| This is the end. | *full stop* or *period* (*American English*) |
| However, | *comma* |
| He waited; | *semi-colon* |
| Here is a list: | *colon* |
| – believe it or not – | *dash* |
| (in brackets) | *... close brackets* |
| well-known | *hyphen* |
| Charlie Brown's | *apostrophe 'S'* |
| What! | *exclamation mark* |
| What? | *question mark* |
| And then ... | *dot dot dot* |
| CAPITALS | |
| *italics* | |
| **bold type** | |
| <u>underlined</u> | |
| 'inverted commas' | *... close inverted commas* |
|   New paragraph | |
| New line | |

!★CAREFUL★! with these types of sentences – look at the grammar and the punctuation:

My father, who is a doctor, lives in the country.
The man who wanted to see you is outside.
He told me that he was waiting.
If you don't look carefully, you won't find it.
You won't find it if you don't look carefully.

Comment on the punctuation rules illustrated here.

## 35.2 In the street ...

Correct the mistakes in punctuation in this dialogue. There are *two* things wrong in each line:

| | |
|---|---|
| Gentleman: | Whats your dog barking at. |
| Lady: | I think, he's barking at you |
| Gentleman: | for God's sake stop it barking |
| Lady: | Don't call it it it's a 'he'. Its alright it's stopped now. |

Gentleman:   Good what's it's name?
Lady:        Although he hasn't got any spot's he's called spot.
Gentleman:   what sort of dog is he
Lady:        Hes a scottish greyhound.
Gentleman:   That's not a very well known breed is it?
Lady:        He's the only one in england as far as I know.
Gentleman:   No wonder, he barks at everyone

## 35.3 On the telephone...

Punctuate this conversation in pairs:

 hallo hallo whos that its me whos me why me of course yes i know its you but who are you ive told you who i am im me i know youre you but i still dont know who you are anyway i dont want to talk to you whoever you are i really want mrs jones who do you want mrs jones mrs jones whos mrs jones why mrs jones lives where you are doesnt she theres no mrs jones here what number do you want i want bournemouth 650283 this is 650823 oh dear i am sorry i must have dialled the wrong number its quite all right ill try dialling again sorry to have troubled you its quite alright goodbye goodbye

Begin like this:

You:    Hallo?
Caller: Hallo ...

## 35.4 Inverted commas

Try this conversation now:

 you know peter said mary i dont think youve heard a word ive just said really i have why were you looking out of the window then peter i thought i heard alans car arriving thats all said peter but i was wrong well im not going to say it all again i did hear you insisted peter i always listen to what you say you know im sure thats alans car this time yes it is well are you going to open the door certainly not hes your brother alright i will then

Begin like this:
'You know ...
and use inverted commas throughout. Start each new speech on a new line.

## 35.5    A punctuation puzzle

*John where Peter had had had had had had had had had the examiner's approval.*

John and Peter had both being doing a grammar exam, where there was a question that required the use of 'had had'. 'Had' was not correct, so …

*John, where Peter had had 'had', had had 'had had'; 'had had' had had the examiner's approval.*

… so John got the mark.

Try the puzzle on a friend.

## 36  Reasons

Giving reasons
Explaining causes and consequences
Making excuses

**36.1**

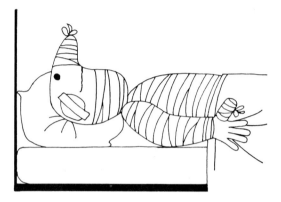

*Why* is he in hospital?
*What's the reason*
*How did it come about that* | he's in hospital?

*Formal writing:*  *Due to* a period of heavy rainfall and patches of dense fog, the road had
become treacherous and visibility was restricted. *Consequently* there was a
collision, in which he was injured.

*Informal speech:*  Well, there was a lot of rain and it was foggy, too. *That's why* the road wa
slippery and he couldn't see very well. *So* he had a crash and got hurt.

Use these structures to express the same ideas:

On account of …      That's the reason …
Owing to …       As a result …

**36.2  More misfortunes**

*In groups*  Can you work out the causes of these disasters and misfortunes:

John failed the exam.          Peter arrived late for the lesson.
Sue didn't get the job.         Michael fell into the sea.
Robert has got a headache.        Little Johnny is crying.

Report your ideas to the other groups (but don't use the word *'because'* !)

### 36.3 Game: 'Feelings'

Each member of the class (or group) selects a different feeling. Pick your feeling:

| | | | |
|---|---|---|---|
| very happy | disappointed | amused | curious |
| depressed | astonished | bored | terrified |
| proud | excited | fascinated | shocked |
| angry | relieved | nervous | impatient |

Now decide secretly *why* you feel that way. Prepare a sentence to say how you feel and put on an appropriate facial expression.

Each student is quizzed by the others to find out *why* he is feeling the way he is. He can only answer 'Yes' or 'No'. Like this:

A: You've won a prize. *Is that the reason* you're very happy?
B: No.
C: I think you've fallen in love. *Is that why* you're happy?
B: No.

### 36.4 Some headlines

*In pairs*  Write sentences to explain the headlines below. For example:
EARTHQUAKE – THOUSANDS HOMELESS
Due to the serious earthquake, thousands of people have been made homeless.

BRIBERY CHARGE PROVED – COUNCILLOR JAILED
WEATHER RUINS HARVEST – FOOD PRICES TO RISE
RIOT AT CONCERT – ROCK GROUP BLAMED
TAXES RISE – PRESIDENT'S LIFE THREATENED
SMOKING – FEWER DEATHS THIS YEAR
LIVERPOOL VICTORY – CITY REJOICES
SHARE PRICES UP – CITY REJOICES
KITTEN RESCUE – TEACHER REWARDED

Compare and discuss your sentences with the others.

### 36.5 Excuses

A: You've broken my window.
B: I'm sorry it happened but | it was an accident.
it was a mistake.
it wasn't my fault.
I'm not to blame.
I did it by mistake.
I didn't do it on purpose.
I didn't mean to do it.
I couldn't help doing it.

A: But | how did it happen?
| why did you do it?
B: Well, you see ... (*reason or excuse*)

Discuss *when* you would use these expressions.

In pairs, following the pattern, act out conversations about these things you have been blamed for:

losing an important letter
burning a hole in a blanket
spilling coffee on the carpet
not coming to class
not repaying the money you borrowed
not making an urgent telephone call

In groups, talk about things you have done which you were blamed for, and things you have done that you are ashamed of.

## 36.6 Making decisions and giving reasons

*In groups*  Solve these problems and state why you have chosen a particular course of action:

1 You have a rifle with one bullet. Two ferocious tigers are about to attack you in the jungle.
2 You are adrift in a lifeboat with two other survivors. The boat will only take one person.
3 You have £1,000 to spend. It must all be spent by midnight. You may not spend it on travel.
4 You are falsely accused of a murder. You think the person you love most dearly is the real murderer.
5 You meet a fairy who gives you three wishes.

### Useful language

My reason for …
One reason I decided to …
Why I decided to …

# 37 Communication

Talking about languages, attitudes to language and communication
Using British gestures and non-verbal signals
Understanding American English lexis and some non-standard British English lexis

## 37.1 Your languages

Answer these questions:

1 What languages do you speak?
2 How well do you speak them?
   a) I'm bi-lingual.
   b) Fluently.
   c) Well enough to make myself understood.
   d) A few words.
3 What foreign language (apart from English) would you most like to learn and why?
4 How many foreigners learn your language?
5 How well do foreign visitors to your country speak your language?
   a) Like native speakers.
   b) Well enough to take part in a discussion.
   c) Enough for shops and hotels.
   d) Not a word.

Discuss your own answers with the others.

## 37.2 Foreign languages

*In pairs*   Here is the sentence: 'I don't understand' in fifteen different languages. Can you work out (or guess) which is which?

a) Un skuptoj
b) Nem értem
c) Je ne comprends pas
d) Mi ne komprenas
e) Ich verstehe nicht
f) No entiendo
g) Ik begrijp het niet
h) Não compreendo
i) Anlamiyorum
j) Nie rozumiem
k) Non capisco
l) En ymmärrä
m) Jag förstår inte
n) Dydw i ddim yn deall
o) Non comprehendo

Choose from these:

| | | | |
|---|---|---|---|
| Latin | Welsh | Turkish | Portuguese |
| French | Swedish | Albanian | Spanish |
| German | Finnish | Esperanto | Italian |
| Hungarian | Dutch | Polish | |

Explain your reasons for each choice to the others.

### 37.3 Talking about communication

Can you use these words?

*Grammar:* structures
*Vocabulary:* idioms, lexis, slang
*Pronunciation:* sounds, stress, intonation, tone of voice
*Gestures:* body language, non-verbal signals
Indo-European, Romance, Germanic ... (what family of languages does your language belong to?) ... Hamito-Semitic, Chinese, Malay

What are the most difficult features of your language for a foreigner to learn?

What have you found most difficult to learn in English?

### 37.4 Tone of voice: expressing mood or attitude

Look at these three sentences:

I love you.
I hate you.
This is an English lesson.

Say each sentence *in your own language* as if you are:

| | | |
|---|---|---|
| angry | bored | happy |
| disgusted | surprised | shocked |
| enthusiastic | sad | afraid |

Mix up the order of moods and get the others in the class to interpret your mood.

#### Useful language

You sound as if ...
It sounds as if ...
You seem to be ...
I'm pretty sure you're ...

Now say the sentences in English and discuss any differences in the tone of voice you use in your own language and in English.

### 37.5 Gestures

What are the British gestures that express these ideas? Demonstrate them!

| | |
|---|---|
| O.K. | Beautiful girl! |
| Drink? | Sit down! |
| Welcome home! | Snob! |
| Don't know. | Telephone! |
| Come here! | Triumph! |
| Go away! | Goodbye! |
| Go straight on. | Stop! |
| Smelly! | Naughty! |

| | |
|---|---|
| Give me it! | Yes! |
| Take it easy! | No! |
| Excellent | I'm angry |
| Chatterbox! | Stupid! |
| Be quiet! | I can't look |
| Time to go! | I beg you! |
| Delicious! | Give me patience! |
| Nasty! | |

How are these gestures different in your country?

## 37.6 Non-verbal signals

What noises are made in Britain to express these feelings?
They are often accompanied by body language, so demonstrate each one:

| | |
|---|---|
| disapproval | be quiet |
| scorn | disgust |
| surprise | excuse me |
| boredom | sympathy |
| liking | annoyance |
| unhappiness | that hurts |
| relief | malicious amusement |
| delicious | |

Would the same non-verbal signals have different meanings in your country?

## 37.7 Understanding American English

Can you translate these words into standard British English?

| | |
|---|---|
| apartment = flat | baggage |
| faucet | vacation |
| elevator | mailman |
| drapes | ZIP code |
| the john | mortician |
| garbage | bar tender |
| closet | public school |
| wash up | movie theater |
| cookie | schedule |
| potato chips | buddy |
| candy | swell ⎫ |
| the Fall | neat ⎬ |
| downtown | cute ⎭ |
| dating | the letter 'Z' |

### 37.8 Understanding non-standard British English

The Scots use a number of dialect words that are not used by the English. What do these mean?

| | | |
|---|---|---|
| a wee house | an advocate | Aye! |
| a bonny bairn | a kirk | to blether |
| a brae | a laddie | a Sassenach |
| a loch | a lassie | |

Children, too (and adults talking to children) use a number of non-standard words. What do these mean?

| | | |
|---|---|---|
| bunny | pussy | baa-lamb |
| moo-cow | choo-choo | doggie |
| din-dins | piggywig | tummy-ache |
| bye-byes | bikkie | wee-wee |
| granny | gee-gee | All gone! |

### 37.9 Game: 'Actions speak louder than words'

A selection of everyday objects (like a mirror, a knife, a glass, a newspaper, a bag of sweets and so on) is brought into the room. The class (or group) sit round in a circle and pass each object round. Each student mimes an action using the object as a 'prop' – it may be used for its usual purpose *or* to represent something else. Each mime should demonstrate a mood or attitude. For example:

Student A picks up the mirror, sniffs it and sneers, then holds it with his fingertips and hands it on to student B.

The others in the circle have to describe the action mimed and the mood demonstrated.

# 38 Purpose

Explaining purposes, precautions

## 38.1 Purposes and precautions

A is rather aggressive:

A: I don't quite see the point of | taking an umbrella.
    What's the point of
    What's the idea of
    Why are you
*or*  What are you taking an umbrella for?
B: It's a good idea to take an umbrella because I want to keep dry.   *Purpose*
*or*  Well, you see, I'm doing it | so as to keep dry.
                         in order to keep dry.
                         in case it starts raining.      *Risk*
                         to avoid getting wet if it rains.   *Risk*

A: So that's why!

Discuss when you would use the expressions and practise with these ideas:

learning English
keeping fit
doing homework
working hard

Continue in pairs, following the pattern, explaining your purpose or the risk you want to avoid:

taking holidays        drinking tea
voting                 going to the bank
arriving on time        having your car serviced
eating a big breakfast

## 38.2 Pointless activities?

In small groups make a short list of pointless things people do.
Then challenge the other groups to answer with appropriate purposes.
For example: shaving

A: What's the point of shaving?
B: Well I shave so as to look smart.
C: And I shave in case people think I look scruffy.

## 38.3   Escape!

*In small groups*   Imagine that you have been on holiday together in a foreign country and suddenly thrown into jail by the police for no just reason. The prison guards have told you that you will be tortured tomorrow at dawn, so you'd like to escape. Plan your escape together – remembering that you need to get right out of the country and that your faces are known to every policeman in the country.

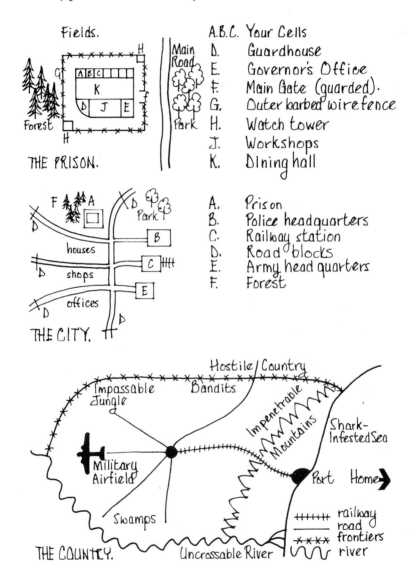

| | |
|---|---|
| A.B.C. | Your Cells |
| D. | Guardhouse |
| E. | Governor's Office |
| F. | Main Gate (guarded). |
| G. | Outer barbed wire fence |
| H. | Watch tower |
| J. | Workshops |
| K. | Dining hall |

THE PRISON.

| | |
|---|---|
| A. | Prison |
| B. | Police headquarters |
| C. | Railway station |
| D. | Road blocks |
| E. | Army head quarters |
| F. | Forest |

THE CITY.

THE COUNTRY.

railway
road
frontiers
river

Explain your plan to the others and be prepared to answer questions like:
'What's the point of doing that?'

Take a vote on the best plan.

# 39  Relationships

Talking about your family, personal relationships and marriage

## 39.1  Your family

This is a family tree:

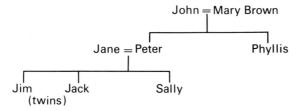

'Mr and Mrs Brown senior have two children. They're called Peter and Phyllis. Phyllis is single, but Peter's married to Jane. They've got three children: twin boys called Jim and Jack, and a little girl called Sally ...'

Draw a family tree of your own family, going back to your grandparents.

In small groups, explain to each other these details about each of the relations in your family:

Your relationship (like: sister-in-law)
Their age
Their character
What they do for a living
Where they live
What they are like

### Useful language

We're not on speaking terms.
We get on very well.
We don't see much of each other.
We often meet.
He always gives me a birthday present.
We spend a lot of time together.

## 39.2 Writing about your family

'Sally's Aunt Phyllis, who isn't married, often spends Christmas with her brother and his family. Jim and Jack, who are twins, are older than their sister.'

Write about your own family in the same way ('*who*' clauses can be used for non-essential by-the-way information).

## 39.3 A church wedding

Describe this picture and the wedding guests in it.

Useful language

Both ... and ...
Neither ... nor ...
All of them are ...
Every one of them is ...
Each of them is ...

Describe a traditional wedding ceremony in your country. Ask your teacher to explain a British one. Ask each other questions.

## 39.4 What do you think about advertisements like this?

# Find your partner now...
# ...the ideal person for love and life

**FREE PARTNER TEST**
FROM BRITAIN'S BIGGEST SCIENTIFIC PARTNER SELECTION SERVICE

**There is nothing more beautiful than a life of harmony and pleasure with another like-minded person. The right one, who is not only an exciting lover but a complementary companion for life. The one you dream of meeting.**

**1. Who is this person your dreams point to?**
Are they dynamic? Are they romantic? Are they film buffs? Do they listen to classical music? Do they prefer parties or a quiet stroll in the park? How tall are they and what colour are their eyes and hair?
However you imagine them they are undoubtedly there.

**2. Who really is your ideal?**
The partner chance analysis tells you in detail the type whose personality, interests and even looks will be ideally complementary to you. It's no secret today that nature can be given more than a little extra assistance with the aid of modern psychology and electronics in the processing of complementary partner profiles. Partner selection quickly edits out from thousands of men and women, the one who is really suited to you.

**3. We invite you to take part in the partner analysis test free and without any obligation.**
Please read the questions carefully, and answer them spontaneously and accurately as this is very important in helping us to assess your data and provide you with an accurate analysis.
We will then let you know your partner selection chances and we expect you will be surprised to find they are more attractive than you ever imagined.
Thousands are taking the new partner test, so why don't you?

**PERSONAL INTERVIEWS**
by mutual arrangement
7 days a week.

**Matchmaker**
International.
25 Kings Road, Sloane Square, London SW3 4RP
Telephone: 01-730 5142 (24 hour service)

**Partner chance test. CONFIDENTIAL**

**1. Your Interests**

**Pastime Interests**
- Playing music, T.V. & Radio
- Parties/dancing, Pubs, clubs etc
- Card games
- Travel./Motoring & Camping
- Politics
- Eating out
- Photography & Science/Maths.

**Arts Interests**
- Ballet, Cinema & Theatre
- Creative writing, Acting
- Social work, Psychology
- Literature & Poetry
- Ecology & History
- Art
- Sculpture

**Sports Interests Profile**
- Outdoor
- Indoor
- Aquatic
- Aerial
- Country

**Musical Interests**
- Progressive Music, Rock etc.
- Classical Music & Opera
- Folk Music & Jazz

**2. Your Personality profile test**

| | |
|---|---|
| ☐ Moody | ☐ Touchy |
| ☐ Anxious | ☐ Restless |
| ☐ Rigid | ☐ Aggressive |
| ☐ Sober | ☐ Excitable |
| ☐ Pessimistic | ☐ Changeable |
| ☐ Reserved | ☐ Impulsive |
| ☐ Unsociable | ☐ Optimistic |
| ☐ Quiet | ☐ Active |
| ☐ Passive | ☐ Sociable |
| ☐ Careful | ☐ Outgoing |
| ☐ Thoughtful | ☐ Talkative |
| ☐ Peaceful | ☐ Responsive |
| ☐ Controlled | ☐ Easygoing |
| ☐ Reliable | ☐ Lively |
| ☐ Even-tempered | ☐ Carefree |
| ☐ Calm | ☐ Leadership |

**3. What would your ideal future relationship be?**
☐ Long lived ☐ Platonic ☐ Physical

**4. Politics:**
I would consider myself to be
☐ Conservative ☐ Other
☐ Socialist ☐ Unconcerned

**5. I would like to meet partners who come from the following social backgrounds:**
☐ Industrial or other workers
☐ Executive and professional classes
☐ Don't mind

**6. Appearance — Build**

| Myself | My choice |
|---|---|

**Physical appearance**

| Myself | My choice |
|---|---|

**7. Confidential personal data**

| | |
|---|---|
| My age is: | My Choice |
| My Height: | My Choice |
| Hair colour: | My Choice |
| Shape: My Choice | |
| Weight: | |
| Eye colour: | My Choice |
| Skin colour: | My Choice |
| Number of Diplomas/ GCE's and level | |
| Degrees | |
| Occupation | |
| Training | |
| Gross monthly Salary or Commission | |

Marital Status
Number of Dependent Children
Number of children living with you or not
Religion
Have you any physical handicap?

**8. Address** Mr/Mrs/Miss
Christian Names ____________
Surname ____________
Street ____________
Town ____________
Post Code ____________
Telephone No. ____________

WK5/79

**Declaration**
I declare that I am unmarried, over 18 and wish to take part in the partner chance test free.

I will be partaking in a test which explains to me the chances of meeting my dream person in the partner circle. The test result and the information on this form will be treated in complete confidence. I furthermore understand that you will send a chance report only at your discretion. I also agree to provide any additional information if reasonably required and if requested. I enclose two first class stamps.

## 39.5 He and she: the stages of a romance (?)

| | | |
|---|---|---|
| *Stage* 1 | chat a girl up | He chatted her up. |
| *Stage* 2 | ask a girl out | He asked her out. |
| | take a girl out | He took her out. |
| *Stage* 3 | good friends | They're good friends. |
| | fond of … | She's fond of him. |
| *Stage* 4 | keen on … | He's keen on her. |
| *Stage* 5 | get on well with … | She gets on well with him. |
| | have a lot in common with … | He has a lot in common with her. |
| *Stage* 6 | going out with … | She's going out with him. |
| *Stage* 7 | get involved with … | He has got involved with her. |
| *Stage* 8 | in love with … | She's in love with him. |
| *Stage* 9 | engaged to … | He's engaged to her. |
| *Stage* 10 | break it off | She's broken it off. |
| | call it off | They've called it off. |
| *Stage* 11 | get married to … | She's got married to him. |
| *Stage* 12 | live together | They live together. |
| *Stage* 13 | go off … | … she's gone off him. |
| *Stage* 14 | walk out on … | She walked out on him. |
| | leave … | She left him. |
| *Stage* 15 | split up | They've split up. |
| | separate | They've separated. |
| *Stage* 16 | divorce | They're divorced. |

In pairs, fill in the gaps in this story. There may be more than one possible expression that makes sense:

Henry wanted to ……………… Harriet ………………, so he chose a moment when they were alone together. She said she'd love to ……………… him and they agreed to go to the cinema. They had a drink after the performance and it was clear they ……………… After a few more evenings out Henry began to ……………… Harriet and before long he realized he had ……………… her. She ……………… him, too, she said. Time passed and for some reason or other they started to ……………… each other. They kept on having rows and it was clear they ………………, so they decided to ……………… and be just ………………

In pairs, describe the developing relationships of some people you know – or fictional characters from a film you've seen or a book you've read.


## 39.6 Marriage

In a Church of England wedding service the clergyman asks the bridegroom this question:

'Wilt thou love her, comfort her, honour, and keep her, in sickness and in health; and forsaking all other, keep her only unto thee, so long as ye both shall live?' He replies: 'I will.'

And he asks the bride:

'Wilt thou obey him, and serve him, love, honour, and keep him, in sickness and in health; and forsaking all other, keep thee only unto him, so long as ye both shall live?' She replies: 'I will.'

In groups, work out a list of more *modern* promises for each partner. Here are two for each to start with.

BRIDEGROOM
I will...
share the housework with my wife
never eat biscuits in bed

BRIDE
I will...
never get fat
always be punctual

**39.7    Ideal marriage**

Write your definition of an ideal marriage. Give examples of the behaviour that would make it ideal.
In groups, show what you have written to the others. Discuss the interesting points.

# 40 Contrast

Stating reservations and counter-arguments
Talking about surprising and unexpected events
Using contrast clauses accurately

## 40.1 Reservations

A: Let's ...                          *Plan*
B: The trouble is ...                 *Reservation*
   The problem is ...
A: That's true, but ...               *Counter-argument*
   But still ...
   That may be so, but ...
   I see what you mean, but ...
B: That's a good point.               *Agree*
*or* I still think that ...            *Disagree*

Discuss when you would use the expressions.

In pairs, follow the pattern using these ideas:

| *Plan* | *Reservation* | *Counter-argument* |
|---|---|---|
| fly to Scotland | expensive | save time |
| Chinese meal | don't like foreign food | new experience |
| new car | very expensive | a year's guarantee |
| buy a house | not enough money | mortgage is cheaper than rent |
| take up ski-ing | dangerous | (your own counter-argument) |
| holiday in November | weather bad | |
| take up jogging | friends will laugh | |
| new job | (your own reservations) | |
| have a party | | |
| (your own plans) | | |

## 40.2 Surprises: using contrast clauses

Useful language

I went for a walk | in spite of the rain.
                  | despite the rain.
I went for a walk | although it was raining.
                  | even though it was raining.
It was raining. | Nevertheless, I went for a walk.
                | In spite of this I went for a walk.

Report the conversations you had in 40.1, using the structures above.

In pairs, use the structures to make sentences from these ideas:

good boy – mother angry
lazy – passed exam
not hungry – big lunch
sunshine – in bed
breakdown – on time
umbrella – dry
played well – lost match

## 40.3   Unexpected things

In small groups, make a list of unexpected things that have happened to each of you. Talk about things like interviews, unexpected meetings, holidays, journeys. When you are ready, describe the events in your list to the other groups and let them summarize what they hear using the structures above.

# 41 Quantity

Expressing quantity, needs and requirements

## 41.1 Essential language

millions of …
far too many …
an enormous number of …
thousands of …
hundreds of …
dozens of …

far too much …
a great amount of …

masses of …
quite a lot of …
plenty of …
ENOUGH
hardly any …
not enough …

several …
a few …
a small number of …
very few …

a little …
a small amount of …
very little …

I could do with some more …
I need some more …
NO … AT ALL
I've run out of …
I haven't got any … left
If only I had some …
I wish I had some …

Use the expressions in *sentences* about these ideas:

| | |
|---|---|
| people | food |
| information | wine |
| cars | holiday |
| books | work |
| news | land |
| facts | countries |

## 41.2 How much?... How many...?

A: I've run out of ...                              *None*
B: How much ...
   How many ... do you need?
A: Oh ...                                            *Quantity required*
B: Can't you make do with ...                        *Smaller quantity*
A: No, that's not enough.                            *Disagree*
*or* Yes, that'll do I suppose.                       *Agree*

In pairs, follow the pattern using these ideas. Be more precise about the quantities this time:

| | | |
|---|---|---|
| money | petrol | stamps |
| cigarettes | writing paper | coffee |
| bread | envelopes | ideas |

## 41.3 Dear Aunt Rachel ...

Fill in the gaps with the 'best' expressions:

Dear Aunt Rachel,

   I'm sorry I didn't thank you for the car you gave me last Christmas, but I was busy. I'm writing now because I ........................ I also ........................ I know you ........................ , so you can afford it. Oh, and ........................ ........................ for my birthday.

   You could send me a cheque if you like, then I can get the things myself and there won't be any mistakes. By the way, ........................ ........................ champagne this month, but some more whisky would be alright,

                          Your loving nephew,
                              Leo

*In pairs*   Play the roles of Aunt Rachel and Leo on the telephone, making the same requests.

## 41.4 What we need ...

*In groups*   Imagine you are the government of a small, very poor island state. Decide what you need to make your lives more pleasant. Then report your needs to the International Monetary Fund committee (everyone else). Invent a suitable name for your country.

## 41.5 What I need ...

What do you need to make your personal life as comfortable as possible? And what can you do without? Tell everyone else after you've made a few notes.

## 42  Crime

Talking about criminal law in your own country
Talking about crime and punishment

### 42.1  English criminal law

When a crime is committed there is a police investigation. The suspect is questioned by the police.

He may then be arrested and charged. And perhaps held in custody.

He appears in a Magistrates' Court. He may be represented by a solicitor. Minor cases are dealt with at this Court.

Serious cases go to the Crown Court, where there is a jury and a judge. The defendant may be represented by a barrister.

The jury finds him guilty or not guilty and the judge will acquit him *or* put him on probation *or* fine him *or* send him to prison.

He can appeal against conviction.

How would the process of law work in your country? What are the differences from the English system? Do you have a jury system?

## 42.2 Visit the court

If you are in Britain, go and visit the local Court. You can find out when they are in session by phone. Look in the phone book under:
'COURTS – Magistrates' Court and Crown Court'

Ring them up and ask:
'When is the Court in session? I'd like to come and watch.'

Go and observe the proceedings for an hour or so.

Report what you saw to the others in the class and compare notes.

## 42.3 Your verdict

*In groups*  What punishment or treatment should be given to these criminals:

1  A well-off housewife takes a bottle of perfume from a department store.  (*Shoplifting*)
2  A husband kills his wife after finding she has been unfaithful.  (*Murder*)
3  A group of men kill five customers in a pub by leaving a bomb there.  (*Terrorism*)
4  A group of schoolboys break all the windows in a telephone box and damage the telephone.  (*Vandalism*)
5  A motorist kills a pedestrian after an evening's drinking.  (*Manslaughter*)
6  An office worker helps himself to pens and paper from his office for his own personal use.  (*Theft*)
7  A group of young men take a woman's handbag after threatening to attack her in a dark street.  (*Mugging*)
8  A motorist parks in a no-parking area and obstructs the traffic so that an ambulance can't get past.  (*Illegal parking*)
9  Two groups of rival football supporters start a battle and are all arrested.  (*Football violence*)
10  A man attacks a girl in a park and has sex with her against her will.  (*Rape*)

Report your group's verdict to the others.
What would actually happen to these offenders in your country?

## 42.4 Crimes

Make a list of all the crimes you can think of.
What is the punishment you recommend for each one?

## 42.5 Talking points

*In groups*  Are the police in your country too hard or too soft? Why?
Is the application of justice too hard or too soft? Talk about the probation system, suspended sentences, the lack of a death penalty.

What reforms would you like to see in the administration of law and order?

### 42.6 'A crime wave'

*In groups*   There has been a series of burglaries, robberies and attacks in this area. You are both worried and angry because not only has your own home been broken into, but two friends of yours have been attacked.

You have decided to form a deputation to the Chief Constable. You are not satisfied with the police's handling of this crime wave. In groups, decide what proposals you intend to make.

When you are ready, go to the Chief Constable (your teacher) and tell him what measures you propose.

# 43  In the news

Talking about a topical event
Reporting what you have read in a newspaper

## 43.1  A topical event

Decide on a topic – an event that is in the news this week from Britain or elsewhere in the
world.
Try to choose something that is controversial.

## 43.2  Questionnaire: ask five people

Ask five people outside class what they think of the topic.
Report the answers to the class, add your own views and discuss.

## 43.3  Background

Describe the background to the event, give a short biography of the people involved.
Try to anticipate the outcome.

## 43.4  Newspapers

Buy two British newspapers of different types and read what they have to say in articles
about the event.
Pay particular attention to the leader or opinion column, too.

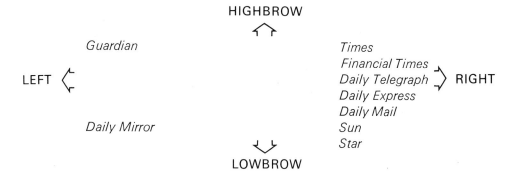

Summarize what you have found out.

Describe the newspapers published in your own country.

## 43.5 Write

Write your own views in leader style.

## 43.6 Newspapers again

Look at the same newspapers you used in 43.4 (or buy some new ones). Split up into groups, each of whom will concentrate on *one* section only of the paper. Depending on the paper, there may be sections on: International News, Home News, Sport, Entertainment, Fashion, The Arts, Business and Finance. There should be enough groups to cover each main section of the paper.

Read your section and prepare a report for the other groups. Say what you think about the articles, too.

Explain the headlines in your section to the other groups.

# 44 Emphasis

Emphasizing the important information in sentences by using emphatic stress, cleft and pseudo-cleft sentences

## 44.1 Who likes what?: The one who . . .

|  | PETER Likes | Dislikes | KATE Likes | Dislikes |
|---|---|---|---|---|
| DRINK | tea | gin | gin | tea |
| FOOD | chips | spaghetti | steak | custard |
| CAR | M.G. | Mini | Ferrari | Ford |
| ANIMAL | cat | snake | cat | worm |
| FILM STAR | Raquel Welch | Elizabeth Taylor | Paul Newman | Raquel Welch |

|  | YOU Like | Dislike |
|---|---|---|
| DRINK |  |  |
| FOOD |  |  |
| CAR |  |  |
| ANIMAL |  |  |
| FILM STAR |  |  |

A: So Peter dislikes tea?
B: No, *Kate* dislikes tea.   (*Emphatic stress*)

A: So Kate likes tea?
B: No, Peter's the one who likes tea.

A: So Kate dislikes gin?
B: No, the one who dislikes gin is Peter.

A: So Peter likes gin?
B: No, it's Kate who likes gin.

Follow the pattern and make up more exchanges about Peter and Kate.
Fill in your own likes and dislikes. Talk about them in the same way.

## 44.2 Who likes what?: What he likes is . . .

| | PETER | | KATE | |
|---|---|---|---|---|
| | *Likes* | *Dislikes* | *Likes* | *Dislikes* |
| COLOUR | blue | brown | brown | black |
| WRITER | Hemingway | Dickens | Austen | Steinbeck |
| HOBBY | do-it-yourself | stamp-collecting | reading | stamp-collecting |
| SPORT | football | squash | tennis | cricket |

| | YOU | |
|---|---|---|
| | *Like* | *Dislike* |
| COLOUR | | |
| WRITER | | |
| HOBBY | | |
| SPORT | | |

A: Does Peter like yellow?
B: No, he likes *blue*.   (*Emphatic stress*)

A: Does Peter dislike green?
B: No, what he dislikes is brown.

A: Does Kate like orange?
B: No, brown is what she likes.

A: Does Kate dislike maroon?
B: No, it's black that she dislikes.

Follow the patterns and make up more exchanges about what they like.
Fill in your own preferences and talk about them in the same way.

## 44.3 What I'm afraid of is . . .

| PETER | | KATE | |
|---|---|---|---|
| *Afraid of* | *Fond of* | *Afraid of* | *Fond of* |
| dogs | cats | mice | horses |
| his father | his mother | her boss | Peter |
| telephoning | TV | the dark | driving |

A: I hear Peter's afraid of cats.
B: No, he's afraid of *dogs*.   (*Emphatic stress*)

A: I understand Peter's fond of goldfish.
B: No, what he's fond of is cats.

A: I've been told Kate's afraid of dogs.
B: No, it's mice that she's afraid of.

A: They say Kate's fond of snakes.
B: No, horses are what she's fond of.

Follow the pattern to talk about their other fears and preferences. Use these words:

| | | |
|---|---|---|
| afraid of | frightened of | keen on |
| terrified of | fond of | crazy about |

Make a list of six of your own fears and likes. Talk about them in the same way.

## 44.4 Test each other

*In pairs* Look at the three lists in 44.1–44.3 first. Then test each other on the information about the characters and yourself. Use the patterns you have practised.


## 44.5 Alternatives

*In pairs* Invent questions from the prompts below and get someone else to reply appropriately, like this:
*Prompt:* red wine or …
A:    Would you like red wine or white wine?
B:    Red wine is what I'd like.
*or*    What I'd like is red wine.

| | | |
|---|---|---|
| yesterday or … | exams or … | London or … |
| Peter or … | your father or … | Mary or … |
| July or … | next week or … | telephone or … |
| a bath or … | cigarettes or … | Christmas or … |
| beer or … | tennis or … | |


## 44.6 More alternatives

*In two teams* Write down on slips of paper a couple of alternatives like the ones in 44.5. For example: fish or meat, classical music or rock music. Then give the slips to the question-master who will shuffle them and give each player a slip. He must then ask an appropriate question (to get a point for his team) and challenge someone on the opposing team to reply (to get a point for *his* team).


## 44.7 Emphasizing times and places

Peter went on a sales tour of Europe, spending a month in each city he visited. This was his itinerary:

| | | | | | |
|---|---|---|---|---|---|
| Jan | Brussels | May | Rome | Sept | Stockholm |
| Feb | Paris | June | Vienna | Oct | Oslo |
| Mar | Lisbon | July | Frankfurt | Nov | Helsinki |
| Apr | Madrid | Aug | Copenhagen | Dec | Amsterdam |

A: So he went to Paris in January?
B: No, Brussels is where he went in January.
A: And he went to Lisbon in February?
B: No, March is when he went to Lisbon.

Continue the conversation, with A making more mistakes and B correcting them.

Talk about the places *you* went last year and when you went there in the same way.

## 44.8   Making your meaning clear

Use the patterns introduced in 44.1–44.3 to show the important information in these sentences. For example:

I've got to see Mr Jones.   (Not Mrs Jones)

I've got to see *Mr* Jones.   (*Emphatic stress*)
*or* The one I've got to see is *Mr* Jones.
*or* *Mr* Jones is the one I've got to see.

I'm going there tomorrow.   (Not today)
The best route from London to Bournemouth is the M3.   (Not the M4)
Shakespeare was born in Stratford-upon-Avon.   (Not Stratford in East London)
I heard the news at 9 o'clock.   (Not 10 o'clock)
There were 500 people there.   (Not 5,000)
I can't swim very well.   (Only a little)
There seems to be something wrong with my radio.   (Not my TV)
It's a long way from here to America.   (Not Africa)
I'm looking forward to going out for a meal.   (Not just a drink)
I've got to go to the dentist's.   (Not the doctor's)

## 45  Dramatic inversion

Telling a story with dramatic emphasis
Using inversion accurately and appropriately

### 45.1  Direction used for dramatic emphasis

In he came …
Out he walked …
Up he got …
Down he fell …
Off he ran …
Back he came …

What is the effect of saying 'In he came' rather than 'He came in'?
How might the sentences above be continued?

Get one of the group to stand up, walk around, go out and come back again. Then narrate what happened excitingly!

### 45.2  Making a dramatic emphasis with word-order changes

When narrating your experiences, these techniques are also useful:

Only after …
Only later …
Only when …,
Not until …
Not only … but also …
Never in my life …
No sooner … than …

Look at these examples:

Only after a long discussion did we manage to reach a decision.
Only later did we realize it was the wrong decision.
Only when we realized, did it seem necessary to change our minds.
Not until the next day did I telephone him.
Not only was he angry, but he also slammed down the phone.
Never in my life have I seen him so upset.
No sooner did I realize this than I apologized.

How would these sentences be spoken *without* this dramatic emphasis?

Make up more similar sentences about the pictures on the next page:

### 45.3 Dramatic inversion

*In pairs or teams*  Write on slips of paper several simple sentences like:
'I listened to the music.'
'The alarm clock went off.'

Then challenge another pair (or team) to use it with a 'dramatic inversion'. They will probably have to *add* ideas to the simple sentence. If they can't do it, you don't get the point unless *you* can!

### 45.4 Your own story

*In groups*  Make notes of an experience you have had that seemed exciting or dramatic. Tell it to the others in your group.

Write the same story.

# 46 Sport

Talking about different sports, stating your likes and dislikes
Describing your favourite sport

## 46.1 Talking about your skills

### Useful language

I'm very good at …
  brilliant at …
  quite good at …
  not bad at …

I've had training in …
  lessons in …

I'm hopeless at …
  very bad at …
  pretty bad at …
  no good at all at …

I'm out of practice in …
I need to brush up my …

Use the expressions to talk about your own skill at these activities:

| Sports | Games | Hobbies |
|---|---|---|
| tennis | chess | knitting |
| football | Monopoly | cooking |
| cricket | bridge | sewing |
| swimming | patience | acting |
| running | | |
| jogging | | |
| rugby | | |
| high jump | | |
| motor racing | | |
| golf | | |
| boxing | | |
| wrestling | | |
| riding | | |

Now think about the past (your schooldays perhaps) and the future (activities you might take up). Talk about them in the same way, like this:

I used to play a lot of football and I was quite good at it.
*or* I'm thinking of taking up tennis and I'm going to have some lessons.

## 46.2 Boasting

In pairs, play one of these roles as you find out about each other's talents:

A: You think you are wonderful. Be arrogant and boastful.
B: You have an inferiority complex.

Use expressions like these:

I wish I was ...
I'm afraid I'm ...
Every time ...
Whenever ...

A: I'm brilliant at football – every time I play I score all the goals!
B: I wish I was good at football – whenever I try to kick the ball I fall over!

Report your best exchange to the others.


## 46.3 Your favourite sports

What sports do you most enjoy playing *and* watching? What do you enjoy about them?
Can you briefly explain the game to someone who is unfamiliar with it? Find out the words
you need to explain it.

**Some useful words**

| | | |
|---|---|---|
| pitch | game | referee |
| field | match | umpire |
| court | first half | |
| course | half-time | |


## 46.4 The best ever ...

Who do you think is or was the world's best ever:

footballer
skier
athlete
boxer
cyclist
gymnast
swimmer
racing-driver
tennis player

What made each of them great?

## 46.5   Questionnaire: ask five people

---

SPORT SURVEY

1. Do you support a football team?  Which one?

2. Do you play any sport now?  Did you use to?

3. Do you watch sport on TV?  Why?

4. Do you have any other spare-time activities (such as fishing or do-it-yourself)?  What pleasure do you get from them?

---

Report your findings, discuss them and give your own answers to the questions.

## 46.6   Talking points

*In groups*   Professional football causes violence on the terraces.
International sport increases chauvinism.
The Olympic Games should be really amateur.
Boxing is barbaric.
So is bull-fighting.
So is hunting.
Gambling on horse races is wrong.
Motor-racing is not a real sport.

Report your discussion to the other groups.

## 46.7   'Olympic Games'

Each member of the class is representing a different country at the Olympic Games in the Marathon. Decide on your country.

1 BEFORE:   You are all having dinner at the Olympic Village the evening before the event.
Talk about how confident you are, what sort of training you have been doing, what sort of weather you are hoping for.
No more than six can sit at each table.

2 AFTER:   Your teacher will give out slips of paper with the results:
one gold medal
one silver medal
one bronze medal
one fourth position
several losers and
several who didn't finish the course

You are having dinner after the event. Talk about the race and your feelings as you eat.

3 BACK HOME:   Be prepared to be interviewed by the Press (everyone else) on your return to your country.

# 47  Written and spoken styles

Using formal written English appropriately
Writing telegrams and letters

## 47.1  Colloquial style and formal style

*a)* 'Well, I think dogs are alright as
companions and so on – you know, they're
ever so faithful and obedient – but they're
just not clever like cats – not unless
they're those dogs that round up sheep
or go out with hunters or something.'

*b)* 'Although the faithfulness and
obedience of dogs makes them good
companions, they frequently lack the
intelligence of cats, unless for example
they are sheepdogs or hunting dogs.'

What are the differences between the two versions?
Why are they different?
As a class, put this conversational text into formal written English:

'Well, it was quite a good book – full of excitement and so on – but, you know, it didn't
really appeal to me. I'm not sure why, maybe it's because of the way it was written – he
was trying to be sort of poetic all the time, not just sticking to the story.'

## 47.2  Write

*In pairs or
small groups*

Now, here are some more pieces of conversational English. Discuss each one in pairs or
small groups, then compose a written version. Read your written versions out to everyone
else.

'Anyway, I got this lovely watch for
Christmas and I'm ever so pleased with
it … it tells you the date and it's got
one of those alarm clock things you can
set so you know you've got to remember
something … it's jolly useful and it
keeps good time, too … oh, and
you don't have to wind it up, either …'

'So this guy came in, right, and he said he wanted a job … well, you don't just come barging in without ringing up or anything … I mean, what are people going to think? … anyway, he said he needed work and we had a chat about his qualifications and what sort of things he'd done before and things like that and in the end, well, he'd sort of sold himself and I said O.K. we'll give you a try for a month.'

'You'll find it's a very useful gadget … it's got all sorts of uses … look you can do this with it and this, and you can even open tins … if you've lost your tin-opener, that is, ha ha … anyway I think you'll find it's a good bargain and if you like you can have two of them for only a pound … that's a saving of about twenty-five per cent, you know.'

'Well, at 8 o'clock we might be going to see this film about whales on BBC 2 I think it is … or is it on the other side? … I'm not sure, anyway we'd like to see it, so if you do drop in I hope you don't mind sitting through that … it'll be quite interesting I think … or you could come later, say about 9, then we could go out for a quick one if you feel like it … anyway we'd like to see you tonight so try and come, won't you?'

'Well, the reading room's getting a bit crowded these days … I mean it's a bit on the small side anyway so on a rainy day you get all these people in sort of sheltering from the rain and some of them don't even have anywhere to sit, believe it or not … anyway, what I'd like to suggest, if we can afford it that is, is that we open up that other room … you know, the one across the corridor … and we could put the newspapers in there – not the magazines, just the papers – and then there'd be less of a crush in the main reading room.'


## 47.3  Authentic speech into writing

Take a piece of recorded colloquial English (from *Functions of English*, for example). Listen to it. Look at the transcript.
Express the same ideas and give the same information in formal written English.

Compare your version with someone else's.


## 47.4  Telegrams and telex messages

What do these messages mean and what is the relationship of the sender and receiver?

```
REGRET DELAYED RAIL STRIKE STOP ARRIVING MONDAY MORNING PLEASE
ARRANGE HOTEL ONE NIGHT STOP HAVE LUNCH MY EXPENSE MONDAY STOP
REGARDS PETER

AMEND BOOKING NAME SMITH STOP AMENDED DATES FOURTH JULY TO
SIXTEENTH INCLUSIVE STOP NOW REQUIRE EXTRA ROOM PLEASE CONFIRM
STOP SMITH

MANY THANKS FOR WEEKEND STOP COMPANY SUPER FOOD AND DRINK
MAGNIFICENT STOP GREATLY ENJOYED OUR CONVERSATIONS STOP LOVE
TO MARY AND KIDS STOP BEST WISHES PETER
```

*In pairs*  Give the same information in a back-to-back 'telephone' conversation.

*In small groups*  Compose letters giving the same information. Show them to the others when you have finished.

## 47.5 Writing telegrams

*In pairs*  In pairs, compose a telegram to send to the next pair. The telegram should require an answer. Send your telegram and reply to the one you receive, asking for further information or clarification.

Repeat the procedure, this time working alone and sending your telegram to someone else.

## 47.6 A letter to the editor of a local newspaper

Sir, There has been a lot of unfair and biased criticism of families who welcome foreign students into their homes. I should like to tell your readers of my own personal experiences, which are not so different from my neighbours' experiences, I might add.

A host family is sent students by the school or college and their home is regularly inspected by the accommodation staff. If a home is below the required standard, the family are removed from the school's accommodation list. Apart from this, the host family is obliged to follow certain rules, as laid down by the school. The problem is that the host family cannot inspect students or refuse to accept the ones who look dirty, unreliable or noisy. And they don't seem to follow any rules at all in their behaviour to the host family. We are often treated like servants or hotel staff, which is rude and bad manners.

The fee paid to a host family only just covers the actual cost of providing meals etc.. A hostess is lucky to make more than a pound or two 'profit' on each student. One has to remember that she has to wash their clothes, allow them to have hot baths, pay for their lighting and the heating in their bedrooms (which is often left on all through the night) and cope with damage to furniture, bedding and carpets (often not discovered till after departure).

Another thing is that most of them do not want to be part of the family. They prefer to be out with other students causing annoyance to local residents in the town centre. They remain in their bedrooms all morning and afternoon if they can, resting before the evening so that they can go out until the early hours of the morning (waking host families up on their return).

Bedrooms become like pigsties. Food, empty bottles and waste paper all goes under the bed (although a waste bin is provided). When taken to task the reply is invariably that they don't understand or that the school has told them they may do as they wish.

How do I know all this? I was a hostess for 10 years and I have suffered. Believe me, every penny made by a host family is hard earned. Not only that, but we have to put up with their complaints about the food, the weather and even our TV programmes. It's time foreign students were taught to be polite and to behave properly, as well as how to speak English!

Yours faithfully,
A PAST SUFFERER
(name and address supplied)

Make notes of the points the writer makes and of any counter-arguments that strike you.

Discuss how you would reply to the letter (by writing to the Editor of the same newspaper). If you could *speak* to the writer, what would you say to her. Act out the scene in pairs, perhaps.

Write a reply to the letter. Show your letter to someone else.

# 48 Word-building

There are seven sections in this unit. They cover the following areas:

**48.1** *Windy*        Building adjectives from nouns, using these suffixes:
-y                -ous
-ed               -al
-ly               -ic

**48.2** *Painful*      Building adjectives from nouns and verbs, using these suffixes:
-ful              -less
-ish              -able
-proof

**48.3** *Unkind*      Building negative adjectives and verbs, using these prefixes:
un-               dis-
in-               non-
im-               mis-
il-               de-
ir-

**48.4** *Intelligence*  Building nouns from adjectives, using these suffixes:
-ence             -ness
-ity              -ment
-ion              (and some important exceptions)
-y

**48.5** *Modernize*    Building causative verbs from adjectives, using these suffixes:
-ize
-en
-ify

**48.6** *Over-dressed*  Building words using these prefixes:
over-             re-
anti-             fellow-
pro-              co-
ex-

**48.7** *Exploration*   Building nouns from verbs to describe actions, using these suffixes:
-ion              -ment
-al               -ance

Students should prepare each section *before* the class, using a dictionary. This will save time in the lesson and help you to remember the words better. It's very important to revise each section the evening *after* practising it to make sure you remember it.

## 48.1 Windy

wind *y*
cloud
snow
water
hair
sand
dust
grass
rock
mood
wool
crunch
chew

mother *ly*
man
coward
world
hour
day
night
week
fortnight
year

curly hair *ed*
red face
blue eyes
talent
skill
experience

poison *ous*
courage
religion
ambition

music *al*
magic
logic
profession
region
culture
history
habit
nation
finance
philosophy
crime

poet *ic*
drama
romance
sympathy
system
idiom
science
hero
specify
emphasize

Make sure you can pronounce and *spell* the adjectives correctly.
Test your memory by covering each column.

**Practice**

1 Use each of the adjectives in as many collocations as you can think of. Like this:

A: When would you use 'windy'?
B: You can have a windy day, or windy weather, or ...

2 Test each other in pairs or small groups on the adjectives. Like this:

A: What's another way of saying there was a lot of wind?
B: It was very windy.

3 Write sentences using the ten words you most want to remember (not the ones you already knew, though!).

4 Refresh your memory at home tomorrow!

5 By the way, we can also use the -*y* ending as a 'diminutive' ending for nouns. Here are some examples. Can you think of any more?

| | |
|---|---|
| bunny | sweetie |
| daddy | Susie |
| drinkie | girlie |
| Johnnie | pussy |
| piggy | doggie |
| mummy | |

## 48.2 Painful

pain *ful*
tune
harm
hope
care
help
use
meaning
colour
power
thought
delight
success
beauty

bullet *proof*
rain
dust
child
fool
rust
water
sound

break *able*
teach
enjoy
profit
accept
rely
avoid
understand

young *ish*
old
strong
green
red
grey
thirty
twenty

tune *less*
pain
harm
hope
care
help
use
meaning
colour
power
thought
cloud
home
child
sound
top
worth
price

Make sure you can spell and pronounce all the adjectives.
Test your memory by covering each column.

**Practice**

1 Test each other in pairs, like this:

   A: What's a way of saying 'fairly young'?
   B: Youngish.

   Do this column by column.

2 Test each other in pairs at a faster pace, moving between columns and giving only the root-word, like this:

   A: Tune!
   B: Tuneless!
   A: And tuneful!

3 Tell a story round the class using the adjectives from the list. When the first player has used one or two of the words, the teacher will pass the story on to the next player (possibly in mid-sentence). The next player then has to continue and so on.

4 Write sentences using the ten words you most want to remember.

5 Refresh your memory at home tomorrow!

## 48.3 Unkind

**un** kind
pleasant
expected
forgettable
predictable
familiar
reliable
comfortable
fair
used
common
likely
qualified
breakable
balanced
certain
friendly

**dis** honest
satisfied
comfort
loyal
obey
appear
prove
approve
advantage

**im** patient
possible
perfect
polite
personal
practical
probable

**in** correct
sincere
complete
sane
visible
tolerant
efficient
expensive
convenient

**ir** responsible
regular
relevant
rational

**il** legal
legible
literate
logical

**non-** European
British
fiction
smoker
member
stick

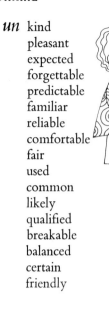

**mis** calculate
understand
manage
pronounce
spell
informed

**un** tie
do
zip
screw
dress
cover
roll
bend
lock
fold

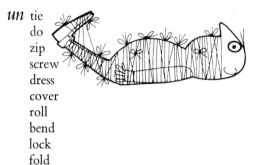

**de** frost
centralize
magnetize
ice
colonize

Test your memory by covering each column.

**Practice**

1 In pairs, test each other on the words listed.
Put each word into a sentence like this:

A: He wasn't very friendly.
B: In other words he was unfriendly.

Jump about in the lists to try and catch each other out.

2 In two teams, test each other on the words. Start with twenty points and lose a point for each mistake. First team to reach zero loses!

3 Try to give rough definitions of the words listed overleaf. It may be effective to use examples sometimes, like this:

*Defrost:* When you defrost something you want it to stop being frozen. Like a frozen chicken.

*Uncomfortable:* When something is uncomfortable – like a wooden chair or clothes that don't fit – you don't really feel at ease.

4 Write sentences using the ten words you most want to remember.

5 Refresh your memory at home tomorrow!

## 48.4 Intelligence

### -ence

| | |
|---|---|
| intelligent | intelligence |
| violent | |
| indifferent | |
| patient | |
| confident | |

### -ion

| | |
|---|---|
| depressed | depression |
| obsessed | |
| fascinated | |
| victimized | |
| satisfied | |

### -ity

| | |
|---|---|
| superior | superiority |
| inferior | |
| stupid | |
| capable | |
| equal | |
| respectable | |
| generous | |
| formal | |
| sensitive | |
| anxious | |
| honest | |
| fluent | |
| brave | |
| artificial | |
| familiar | |
| original | |

### -ness

| | |
|---|---|
| happy | happiness |
| kind | |
| selfish | |
| clever | |
| mean | |
| friendly | |
| quiet | |
| attractive | |
| nervous | |
| dull | |
| great | |
| tall | |
| slim | |

### -ment

| | |
|---|---|
| disappointed | disappointment |
| embarrassed | |
| amazed | |
| amused | |
| encouraged | |
| discouraged | |
| astonished | |

### *Exceptions*

| | |
|---|---|
| strong | strength |
| wise | wisdom |
| bored | boredom |
| hungry | hunger |
| thirsty | thirst |
| proud | pride |
| delighted | delight |
| expert | expertise |
| high | height |
| diplomatic | diplomacy |
| hypocritical | hypocrisy |

Make sure you can spell and pronounce the words correctly. Be particularly careful about word-stress.

Test your memory by covering up each column.

## Practice

1 As a quick check in pairs or groups mask the right-hand column of each list and test each other on the nouns.

2 In groups or teams challenge each other to respond interestingly to sentences like these:

A: It's important to be intelligent, isn't it?
B: Oh yes, intelligence is a very important thing.

B: It's unnecessary to be violent, isn't it?
A: Yes, there's too much violence in the world today.

Jump about in the lists to make things unpredictable!

3 Again in groups or teams, ask each other questions like these:

A: What exactly is intelligence?
B: If you are intelligent you have a lot of brains.

B: What is violence?
A: If you are violent, you attack people.

Use the adjective in the answer.

4 Write sentences using the ten words you most want to remember.

5 Refresh your memory at home tomorrow!

## 48.5 Modernize

### -ize

modern  modernize
central
American
popular
sterile
legal
rational

### -en

sharp  sharpen
flat
hard
tight
loose
soft
sweet
thick
deep
wide
deaf
moist
strong

### -ify

afraid  terrify
simple
pure
electric
clear

warm  warm
cool
dry
wet
calm
blind
narrow
hot

### And

high  raise, lift
low   lower, drop

Test your memory by covering up each column.

**Practice**

1 Ask each other questions like this:

    A: So they made their house more modern?
    B: That's right, they modernized it.

2 Test each other in pairs with questions like these:

    A: What can you sharpen?
    B: You can sharpen a knife or scissors.

    B: What can you warm?
    A: You can warm food or a room.

3 Write sentences using the ten words you most want to remember.

4 Refresh your memory at home tomorrow!

## 48.6 Over-dressed

**over-** dressed
excited
confident
eager
sensitive
emotional
cautious
crowded
emphasize
heat
praise
load
sleep
weight
privileged
simplify
eat
populated
charge
exposed
rated
worked
enthusiastic

**ex-** officer
teacher
student
wife
husband
president
film-star

**re** heat
cook
write
organize
build
arrange
marry
appear
print
unite

**anti-** war
British
communist
government
American

**pro-** government
British
communist
American

**fellow-** countryman
player
Englishman
worker
student
passenger

**co-** driver
owner
chairman
director
(workmate
classmate
teammate)

Test your memory by covering up each column.

## Practice

1 Ask each other questions like this:

A: He's too enthusiastic.
B: In other words, he's over-enthusiastic.

B: He doesn't like the Americans.
A: In other words, he's anti-American.

2 Decide *when* you would use the words. Like this:

A: Over-dressed.
B: She was over-dressed – she was wearing all her diamonds and a long black dress at the supermarket.

B: Ex-officer.
A: He's an ex-officer – he used to be in the army, but now he's retired.

3 Write sentences using the ten words you most want to remember.

4 Refresh your memory at home tomorrow!

## 48.7 Exploration

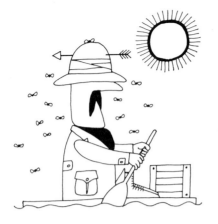

### -al

| propose | proposal |
|---------|----------|
| arrive | |
| survive | |
| refuse | |
| remove | |
| deny | |

### -ion

| explore | exploration |
|---------|-------------|
| receive | |
| classify | |
| deceive | |
| include | |
| subscribe | |
| complete | |
| hesitate | |
| oppose | |
| form | |
| repeat | |
| specify | |
| specialize | |
| combine | |
| cancel | |
| predict | |
| expand | |
| admit | |
| convert | |
| contribute | |
| alter | |
| contradict | |
| consume | |
| discuss | |
| inform | |
| persuade | |
| pronounce | |
| qualify | |
| suspect | |

### judge *ment*

invest
announce
arrange
develop
require

### perform *ance*

resist
disappear
assist

Make sure you can spell and pronounce the nouns correctly.
Test your memory by covering up each column.

**Practice**

1 In two teams, test each other on the words. Start with twenty points and lose a point for each mistake. First team to reach zero loses!

2 Decide *when* you would use the nouns overleaf. For example:

A: Exploration.
B: The exploration of an unknown region or the moon.

B: Proposal.
A: A proposal of marriage, or a proposal like a suggestion.

3 Write sentences using the ten words you most want to remember.

4 Refresh your memory at home tomorrow!

## 49 Word + preposition

Using verb + preposition combinations and adjective and noun + preposition combinations accurately

The main problem with non-literal prepositions is simply remembering them. This unit presents the most useful combinations laid out for home-study. Only the 'Compare your sentences' section needs to be done in class.

**49.1** **A–B**

Write an ending to each of these sentences after filling in the missing prepositions:

| | | |
|---|---|---|
| He apologized | for | |
| I'm not accustomed | | |
| I can't approve | | |
| He was accused | | |
| He was ashamed | | |
| Do you agree | | |
| He seemed annoyed | | |
| We argued all night | | |
| He was astonished | | |
| Are you aware | | |
| What's your attitude | | |
| I'm rather anxious | | |
| What's the advantage | | |
| I believe | | |
| He boasted to us | | |
| You can't blame me | | |
| That car belongs | | |
| I borrowed it | | |

1 Compare your sentences with the other students.
2 Use a thin strip of paper (or a thick pen) to cover up the centre column. Test your memory.
3 Cover up the prepositions and the endings. Test your memory.
4 Cover up the first column only. Test your memory.

**49.2    C–D**

Write an ending to each of these sentences after filling in the missing prepositions:

| | |
|---|---|
| He's capable | of |
| Congratulations | |
| She's crazy | |
| Try to concentrate | |
| The police charged him | |
| The garage charged him £50 | |
| They're always complaining | |
| Give me your comments | |
| You'll have to choose | |
| My family consists | |
| This is characteristic | |
| I disagree | |
| I disapprove | |
| I'm dissatisfied | |
| He was a bit doubtful | |
| Cheers! Let's drink | |
| There's been a delay | |
| We eventually decided | |
| I've had a little difficulty | |

1 Compare your sentences with the other students.
2 Use a thin strip of paper (or a thick pen) to cover up the centre column. Test your memory.
3 Cover up the prepositions and the endings. Test your memory.
4 Cover up the first column only. Test your memory.
5 Look back to 49.1 to refresh your memory.

**49.3    E–H**

Write an ending to each of these sentences after filling in the missing prepositions:

| | |
|---|---|
| He was very enthusiastic | about |
| I'm feeling excited | |
| I have a lot of experience | |
| I feel quite envious | |
| I'm an expert | |
| Excuse me | |
| I don't feel | |
| How do you feel | |
| I'm quite fond | |
| I'm fed up | |
| Forgive me | |
| They're famous | |
| We forgot | |
| I'm frightened | |
| She's friendly | |
| He was found guilty | |
| That tie doesn't go | |

He's always grumbling
She was gentle
Have you heard
There's no hope

1 Compare your sentences with the other students.
2 Use a thin strip of paper (or a thick pen) to cover up the centre column. Test your memory.
3 Cover up the prepositions and the endings. Test your memory.
4 Cover up the first column only. Test your memory.
5 Look back to 49.2 and refresh your memory.

**49.4 I–O**

Write an ending to each of these sentences after filling in the missing prepositions:

I'm very interested | in |
Please don't interfere
She insisted
I'd like some information
I have no intention
She's very involved
Have you heard the joke
She's always kind
I know a lot
It's rude to laugh
Don't ever lend money
Our team lost
He's taken a liking
My mother looks
I'm going on holiday – can you look
Last year he got married
Where are you going?   Are you making
What's the matter
Their son was named
Take no notice
Have you heard any news
What's your opinion
I object

1 Compare your sentences with the other students.
2 Use a thin strip of paper (or a thick pen) to cover up the centre column. Test your memory.
3 Cover up the prepositions and the endings. Test your memory.
4 Cover up the first column only. Test your memory.
5 Look back to 49.3 and refresh your memory.

**49.5　P–Q**

Write an ending to each of these sentences after filling in the missing prepositions:

| | | |
|---|---|---|
| I'm very pleased | with | |
| I was presented | | |
| I'm a bit puzzled | | |
| He's very proud | | |
| How much did you pay | | |
| They provided him | | |
| He protested | | |
| I couldn't ever part | | |
| They prevented him | | |
| He was punished | | |
| It's time to prepare | | |
| I'm pessimistic | | |
| He's very popular | | |
| He needs protection | | |
| I'm well qualified | | |

1　Compare your sentences with the other students.
2　Use a thin strip of paper (or a thick pen) to cover up the centre column. Test your memory.
3　Cover up the prepositions and the endings. Test your memory.
4　Cover up the first column only. Test your memory.
5　Look back to 49.4 and refresh your memory.

**49.6　R–S**

Write an ending to each of these sentences after filling in the missing prepositions:

| | | |
|---|---|---|
| He's much respected | for | |
| What is the result | | |
| Who's responsible | | |
| I've read a report | | |
| What's your reaction | | |
| 'Moon' rhymes | | |
| You can't rely | | |
| There's no room here | | |
| Try to get rid | | |
| Are you related | | |
| Nobody's safe | | |
| She's in bed suffering | | |
| I can't work out the solution | | |
| I'm suspicious | | |
| He succeeded | | |
| If he's angry, just smile | | |
| I feel sorry | | |
| I've made a study | | |
| Are you serious | | |
| She was sympathetic | | |

175

I'm sick
They saved him
AA stands

1 Compare your sentences with the other students.
2 Use a thin strip of paper (or a thick pen) to cover up the centre column. Test your memory.
3 Cover up the prepositions and the endings. Test your memory.
4 Cover up the first column only. Test your memory.
5 Look back to 49.5 and refresh your memory.

## 49.7 T–Z

Write an ending to each of these sentences after filling in the missing prepositions:

He's just like his father – he takes | after
He was talked
He was talked
Stop talking
I'm tired
There should be a tax
What's the trouble
I've been thinking
What's the use
I can't get used
There are thousands of victims
I've already warned you
Don't worry
What's wrong
She has a great zest

1 Compare your sentences with the other students.
2 Use a thin strip of paper (or a thick pen) to cover up the centre column. Test your memory.
3 Cover up the prepositions and the endings. Test your memory.
4 Cover up the first column only. Test your memory.
5 Look back to 49.6 and refresh your memory.

6 Look back to 49.1–49.5 and check that you still remember everything!

## 50 Preposition + noun

Using preposition + noun combinations accurately

The main problem with these selected useful phrases is memorizing them.
The columns help you to do this on your own at home.
Only the 'Discuss' part needs to be done in class.

### 50.1 A–B

Discuss when you would use these expressions:

| | |
|---|---|
| I think we're all | agreement. |
| I didn't mean to do it, it happened | accident. |
| I'm afraid you'll have to pay | advance. |
| His English is good but he speaks | an accent. |
| Hallo! I haven't seen you | ages. |
| He's 15, he can't drink beer because he's | age. |
| There are several points | the agenda. |
| I was welcomed | open arms. |
| The news of their marriage came | the blue. |
| We've all got problems – we're all | the same boat. |
| He's got his exam | the brain. |
| They worked twelve hours | a break. |
| He has gone abroad | business. |
| He's not here, but I can sign | his behalf. |
| He didn't hear because I said it | my breath. |
| I've been running, I'm | breath. |

1 Cover up the middle column and try to remember the prepositions.
2 Cover up the last two columns and try to remember the phrases.
3 Cover up the first column and make up an appropriate beginning for each sentence.

### 50.2 C–D

Discuss when you would use these expressions:

| | |
|---|---|
| We didn't arrange to meet – we met | chance. |
| Let's go to a different bar | a change. |
| Tell me about it – get it | your chest. |
| She's a day-dreamer – she's always | the clouds. |
| You don't look well – you're a bit | colour. |
| They haven't got much | common. |

| Listen, I'm telling you this | confidence. |
| Please keep that dog | control. |
| We must pass the exam | all costs. |
| General Roberts is | command. |
| Mr Harris's deputy is | charge. |
| I can't eat very much, I'm | a diet. |
| Tell me about it. Don't keep me | the dark. |
| Don't be old-fashioned! Keep | date. |
| It's too difficult – I'm | my depth. |
| We haven't decided yet, the matter's still | discussion. |
| Policemen aren't allowed to drink | duty.  |

1 Cover up the middle column and try to remember the prepositions.
2 Cover up the last two columns and try to remember the phrases.
3 Cover up the first column and make up an appropriate beginning for each sentence.
4 Look back to 50.1 to refresh your memory.

## 50.3  E–G

Discuss when you would use these expressions:

| I'm a bit tense – I'm rather | edge. |
| I've got nothing to do – I'm | a loose end. |
| It was a good film but very sad | the end. |
| I found it hard to make up my mind, but I decided | the end. |
| I support the idea. I'll vote | favour. |
| You must be there at 9 o'clock | fail. |
| Sound the alarm! The building's | fire. |
| The building's | flames. |
| Spring is here! The trees are | flower. |
| It's a bad photo – it's all | focus. |
| I didn't drive here. I came | foot. |
| They didn't win because they weren't | form. |
| I could see what sort of man he was | a glance. |
| He's got a permanent job – he's here | good. |
| I'd say there were 5,000 people there | a guess.  |

1 Cover up the middle column and try to remember the prepositions.
2 Cover up the last two columns and try to remember the phrases.
3 Cover up the first column and make up an appropriate beginning for each sentence.
4 Look back to 50.2 to refresh your memory.

## 50.4  H–K

Discuss when you would use these expressions:

| You have to learn these phrases | heart. |
| The two of them were walking hand | hand. |
| I don't know exactly – I can't tell you | hand. |
| Now grandfather's in hospital, he's | good hands. |

| | | |
|---|---|---|
| What a crazy idea! He must be | | his head. |
| He is 1.80 metres | | height. |
| These bicycles are | | hire. |
| They're in Bournemouth | | holiday. |
| You can hear the radio news every hour | | the hour. |
| He went to a night club and got home | | the small hours. |
| These drinks are free – they're | | the house. |
| He was getting married, so we held a party | | his honour. |
| Work hard for the exam – it's | | your own interest. |
| A loan from a bank has to be repaid | | interest. |
| Crimes like mugging are | | the increase. |
| The factory closed down, so he's | | a job. |
| There has been no news yet | | my knowledge.  |

1  Cover up the middle column and try to remember the prepositions.
2  Cover up the last two columns and try to remember the phrases.
3  Cover up the first column and make up an appropriate beginning for each sentence.
4  Look back to 50.3 to refresh your memory.

**50.5   L–M**

Discuss when you would use these expressions:

| | | |
|---|---|---|
| I've been waiting – here you are | | last. |
| There's a dangerous criminal | | large. |
| I must know the answer by Friday | | the latest. |
| There were 5,000 people there | | least. |
| He told us the story of his life | | great length. |
| This book is 120 pages | | length. |
| I can't see to read – you're standing | | my light. |
| It doesn't actually say so, but I've been reading | | the lines. |
| It's not my book – I've got it | | loan. |
| I didn't know what to say – I was | | a loss. |
| I won't charge anything – I'll do it | | love. |
| Your order's not ready yet, you're | | luck. |
| Bill and John are related | | marriage. |
| Yes, certainly, I'll help you | | all means. |
| I'm a bit quiet because I've got a lot | | my mind. |
| I don't know what to do – I'm | | two minds. |
| I didn't mean to do it, I did it | | mistake. |
| She's wearing black because she's | | mourning. |
| I don't feel like doing it, I'm not | | the mood. |

1  Cover up the middle column and try to remember the prepositions.
2  Cover up the last two columns and try to remember the phrases.
3  Cover up the first column and make up an appropriate beginning for each sentence.
4  Look back to 50.4 to refresh your memory.

## 50.6 N–P

Discuss when you would use these expressions:

| | |
|---|---|
| He knows every one of his students | name. |
| Yet again South Africa is | the news. |
| It's free – you can have it | nothing. |
| She posed for the photographs | the nude. |
| I wish you'd do your homework | once. |
| They went into the room one | one. |
| The book you wanted is still | order. |
| Make sure all your clothes are | order. |
| The lift and the escalator are | order. |
| With this toothache I'm really | pain. |
| We're expecting a visit from Her Majesty | person. |
| Among all those famous people I felt | place. |
| It seems alright in theory but it won't work | practice. |
| The book I need for my lecture is | print. |
| I refuse to apologize for it | principle. |
| I'm not totally sure but I agree | principle.  |

1 Cover up the middle column and try to remember the prepositions.
2 Cover up the last two columns and try to remember the phrases.
3 Cover up the first column and make up an appropriate beginning for each sentence.
4 Look back to 50.5 to refresh your memory.

## 50.7 Q–R

Discuss when you would use these expressions:

| | |
|---|---|
| I can't allow it – it's completely | the question. |
| I heard about it | the radio. |
| People questioned in the survey are selected | random. |
| The kidnappers held their hostages | ransom. |
| My car's in the garage – it's | repair. |
| The next record is being played | request. |
| Open three bottles and keep the rest | reserve. |
| It's not perfect, but it's good | some respects. |
| You do the cooking and I'll wash up | return. |
| After the shooting of the terrorist a hostage was killed | revenge. |
| They are wrong but they believe they're | the right. |
| Their marriage is | the rocks. |
| The weather in August is wetter | a rule. |
| It may seem unpleasant, but it'll do good | the long run. |
| Ten years in the same job! I think I'm | a rut.  |

1 Cover up the middle column and try to remember the prepositions.
2 Cover up the last two columns and try to remember the phrases.
3 Cover up the first column and make up an appropriate beginning for each sentence.
4 Look back to 50.6 to refresh your memory.

Discuss when you would use these expressions:

| | |
|---|---|
| The survivors of the Titanic reached New York | safety. |
| I know you don't want to, but please do it | my sake. |
| Because of the bad weather, building is | schedule. |
| It's very difficult learning a language | scratch. |
| You can't get spinach now, it isn't | season. |
| I was going to Spain – but I think I'll go to France | second thoughts. |
| He was about to kill her so she shot him | self-defence. |
| He's getting married tomorrow – I'd hate to be | his shoes. |
| His real name's Robert, but we call him Rob | short. |
| This year there are several new models | show. |
| I don't know his name, but I know him | sight. |
| You can't see it from here because it's | sight. |
| I hadn't booked a theatre ticket, I just went there | spec. |
| If you need help, we have a representative | the spot. |
| I've got to get that job, my whole future is | stake. |
| We have some nice new sandals | stock. |
| There are going to be problems – there's trouble | store. |
| There's been a dispute and the staff are | strike. |
| I tried several times to start my car but | success. |
| The Chief of Police can't be guilty – he's | suspicion. |
| When we arrived at the party it was | full swing.  |

1　Cover up the middle column and try to remember the prepositions.
2　Cover up the last two columns and try to remember the phrases.
3　Cover up the first column and make up an appropriate beginning for each sentence.
4　Look back to 50.7 to refresh your memory.

Discuss when you would use these expressions:

| | |
|---|---|
| I haven't got the record, but I've got it | tape. |
| I didn't like that joke, I thought it was | bad taste. |
| You shouldn't believe everything you see | television. |
| We used to hate each other but now we're | good terms. |
| It won't work in practice although it looks good | theory. |
| I can only serve one customer | a time. |
| I don't remember the fifties, they were | my time. |
| I don't often smoke, but I do | time to time. |
| I'm not too late, am I? I'm sure I got here | time. |
| He arrived early for the concert – he arrived | good time. |
| He got here very quickly – he got here | no time at all. |
| You must arrive punctually – you must be | time. |
| You should read the paper, you're a bit | the times. |
| He's in court tomorrow – he's | trial. |

| | | |
|---|---|---|
| Don't ask me to sing – I can't sing | | tune. |
| Send me a postcard – let's keep | | touch. |

1 Cover up the middle column and try to remember the prepositions.
2 Cover up the last two columns and try to remember the phrases.
3 Cover up the first column and make up an appropriate beginning for each sentence.
4 Look back to 50.8 to refresh your memory.

## 50.10  U–W

Discuss when you would use these expressions:

| | | |
|---|---|---|
| Many British school-children go to school | | uniform. |
| A book like that is useless – it's | | no use. |
| I'm afraid all the machines are | | use. |
| He tried to avoid hitting the tree, but his efforts were | | vain. |
| These old manuscripts are | | great value. |
| She wrote me a whole letter | | verse. |
| When are your new paintings | | view? |
| I don't live here, I'm just here | | a visit. |
| The countries are no longer | | war. |
| The government inspector arrived | | warning. |
| It wasn't your fault, but you are to blame | | a way. |
| I wish he'd leave – he's always | | the way. |
| We've started work – work is now | | way. |
| You don't look very well – you look a bit | | the weather. |
| Your luggage must not be more than 20 kg | | weight. |
| I'm not going to settle down there, but I'll stay there | | a while. |
| The corridor is just over 2 metres | | width. |
| You can't translate idioms word | | word. |
| Please confirm your reservation | | writing. |

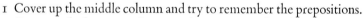

1 Cover up the middle column and try to remember the prepositions.
2 Cover up the last two columns and try to remember the phrases.
3 Cover up the first column and make up an appropriate beginning for each sentence.
4 Look back to 50.9 to refresh your memory.

5 Look back to 50.1–50.8 to end with.

# Key 🔑

## 1.1 What's the weather like?

There isn't a cloud in the sky.
The sun's shining.
It looks a wonderful day.
Do you think this sunshine will last?

It's pouring with rain.
We'll get soaked if we go out.
It's just a shower.
We'd get drenched if we went out.

It looks like rain.
The sun might break through later.
It's clouded over again.
It doesn't look too promising.
Those clouds look rather ominous.

It's snowing quite heavily.
It's bitterly cold.
I hope we aren't cut off!
It's not settling.

## 2.2 'Mysteries'

1 She had hiccups and wanted the water to cure it. It didn't work. The barman gave her a shock by producing the gun; this cured it and she was grateful.
2 He was a parachutist whose parachute failed to open.
3 She had been kept awake by the guest in the next hotel room snoring. The phone call woke him up and she put the receiver down.
4 He hanged himself by standing on a block of ice until it melted.
5 He killed himself. He was the smallest man in the world and was very proud of it. He killed himself because he thought he was growing, because the other man (the second smallest man in the world) had sawn a little piece off the stick he used to measure himself with.

## 3.10 Clothing

| USA | | GB |
|---|---|---|
| suspenders | = | braces |
| vest | = | waistcoat |
| pants | = | trousers |
| necktie | = | tie |
| shorts | = | underpants |
| panti-hose | = | tights |
| sneakers | = | plimsolls, gym shoes |
| tuxedo | = | dinner jacket |

**4.8 'Call me!'**

| USA | | GB |
|---|---|---|
| Call me! | = | Phone me, ring me (up) |
| an unlisted number | = | an ex-directory number |
| Central | = | Exchange |
| to make a collect call person to person | = | transferred charge *or* reverse charge personal call |
| station to station | = | not a personal call |
| Are you through? | = | Have you finished? |

**7.2 Can you use these words?**

| | |
|---|---|
| scriptwriter | current affairs |
| cameraman | commercials |
| actor | crime series |
| actress | soap opera |
| | serial |
| | comedy show |

**8.7 Common abbreviations**

| | | | | | |
|---|---|---|---|---|---|
| RSVP | = | Please reply to this invitation | P.T.O. | = | Please turn over |
| etc. | = | et cetera, and so on | Ltd. | = | Limited |
| c/o | = | care of | & Co. | = | and Company |
| approx. | = | approximately | v. | = | versus |
| p.p. | = | signed on behalf of | P.S. | = | postscript |
| i.e. | = | that is | V.I.P. | = | Very Important Person |
| e.g. | = | for example | Gt | = | Great |

| | | | | | |
|---|---|---|---|---|---|
| Ave. | = | Avenue | A.D. | = | Anno Domini |
| Rd | = | Road | B.C. | = | Before Christ |
| St | = | Street | a.m. | = | in the morning |
| Gdns | = | Gardens | p.m. | = | in the afternoon or evening |
| Sq. | = | Square | M.P. | = | Member of Parliament (or Military Police) |
| Pk | = | Park | | | |
| Cres. | = | Crescent | | | |

| | | |
|---|---|---|
| BBC | = | British Broadcasting Corporation |
| VAT | = | Value Added Tax |
| TUC | = | Trades Union Congress |
| AA | = | Automobile Association (or Alcoholics Anonymous) |
| RAC | = | Royal Automobile Club |
| PC | = | Police Constable |
| EEC | = | European Economic Community (the Common Market) |

### 9.3  Traffic signs

1. No overtaking
2. No U turns
3. 40 m.p.h. speed limit
4. End of speed limit
5. Stop
6. Give way
7. No entry
8. School-children crossing
9. No motor vehicles
10. Quayside or river bank
11. Bend
12. Road works
13. Change to opposite carriageway
14. Right-hand lane closed
15. Slippery road
16. Low-flying aircraft
17. Cattle
18. Wild animals
19. Horses
20. Ford (river crossing)
21. Pedestrian crossing
22. Traffic lights
23. Hump bridge
24. Uneven road
25. Road narrows
26. End of dual carriageway
27. Cross roads
28. Roundabout
29. Traffic merges from left
30. Traffic joins from right
31. Two-way traffic
32. Go for traffic turning left
33. Left-hand lane – left turn only
34. No waiting at any time
35. 20 minutes waiting only
36. No through road
37. Keep left
38. Pass either side
39. Bicycles only
40. Ahead only
41. Turn left
42. Turn left ahead
43. (on a motorway) 50 m.p.h. speed limit
44. (on a motorway) lane closed ahead
45. (on a motorway) road clear

### 9.10  Transportation

| USA | | GB |
|---|---|---|
| gas pedal | = | accelerator |
| hood | = | bonnet |
| trunk | = | boot |
| fender | = | wing |
| a flat | = | a flat tyre or puncture |
| sedan | = | saloon car |
| station wagon | = | estate car |
| truck | = | lorry or truck |
| streetcar | = | tram |
| cab | = | taxi |
| bus | = | bus *or* coach |
| trailer | = | caravan |
| a one-way ticket | = | a single |
| a round trip ticket | = | a return |
| divided highway | = | dual carriageway |
| freeway | = | motorway |
| turnpike | = | toll motorway |
| sidewalk | = | pavement |
| crosswalk | = | pedestrian crossing |
| pavement | = | road surface |
| 'Can you give me a ride?' | = | 'Can you give me a lift?' |
| YIELD | = | GIVE WAY |

## 16.3 Medical problems

| | *Mild* | *Extreme* |
|---|---|---|
| | I feel a bit off colour. | I think I'm dying. |
| | I feel a bit under the weather. | I feel absolutely rotten. |
| headache | I've got a bit of a headache. | I've got a splitting headache. |
| backache | My back's giving me a bit of trouble. | My back's killing me. |
| feeling sick | I feel a bit queasy. | I think I'm going to throw up. |
| sore throat | My throat's a bit dry. | I can hardly speak. |
| cough | I've got a tickle in my throat. | I can't stop coughing. |
| stiffness | I'm a bit stiff. | I can't move. |
| catarrh | I'm a bit stuffed up. | I can hardly breathe. |
| insomnia | I'm having a bit of trouble sleeping. | I didn't sleep a wink last night. |
| toothache | This tooth's playing up a bit. | This tooth's giving me hell. |
| chest pains | My chest hurts a bit. | I've got stabbing pains in my chest. |

## 18.9 'Jumbo'

Get the elephant into the boat. Mark the waterline with paint. Get the elephant out of the boat. Weigh the amount of sand it takes to fill one bucket. Fill up the boat with bucketfuls of sand, counting the number it takes to fill it till the painted line reaches the waterline. Multiply the number of bucketfuls by the weight of one bucketful and the answer is the weight of the elephant.

## 21.1 Happy?

| | | | |
|---|---|---|---|
| cheerful | fed up | in a bad temper | nervous |
| in a good mood | down in the dumps | moody | anxious |
| on good form | depressed | grumpy | apprehensive |
| on top of the world | desperate | in a bad mood | scared |
| jolly | | | worried |

## 23.1 Nationalities

John comes from England.
He's an Englishman.
He has a British passport.
The English speak English.

Jock comes from Scotland.
He's a Scotsman.
He has a British passport.
The Scots speak English, but some also speak Gaelic.

Paddy comes from Ireland.
He's an Irishman.
He has an Irish passport.
The Irish speak English.

Taffy comes from Wales.
He's a Welshman.
He has a British passport.
The Welsh speak English, but many also speak Welsh.

## 23.2 Trafalgar Square

| | | | |
|---|---|---|---|
| A | = | Austria | (Vienna) |
| B | = | Belgium | (Brussels) |
| CH | = | Switzerland | (Berne) |
| CS | = | Czechoslovakia | (Prague) |
| D | = | Germany | (Bonn) |
| DK | = | Denmark | (Copenhagen) |
| E | = | Spain | (Madrid) |
| F | = | France | (Paris) |
| GR | = | Greece | (Athens) |
| H | = | Hungary | (Budapest) |
| I | = | Italy | (Rome) |
| IRL | = | Ireland | (Dublin) |
| N | = | Norway | (Oslo) |
| NL | = | Holland | (The Hague) |
| P | = | Portugal | (Lisbon) |
| PL | = | Poland | (Warsaw) |
| S | = | Sweden | (Stockholm) |
| SF | = | Finland | (Helsinki) |
| TR | = | Turkey | (Ankara) |
| YU | = | Yugoslavia | (Belgrade) |

## 23.3 International airlines

| Airline | Country | Airport |
|---|---|---|
| Air Algerie | Algeria | Algiers |
| Aeroflot | Soviet Union (Russia) | Moscow |
| Aerolineas Argentinas | Argentina | Buenos Aires |
| Aeromexico | Mexico | Mexico City |
| Air Canada | Canada | Toronto |
| Air India | India | Delhi |
| Air New Zealand | New Zealand | Auckland |
| Egyptair | Egypt | Cairo |
| El Al | Israel | Tel Aviv |
| Garuda | Indonesia | Djakarta |
| Iran Air | Iran | Tehran |
| JAL | Japan | Tokyo |
| Kuwait Airways | Kuwait | Kuwait |
| Libyan Arab Airlines | Libya | Tripoli |
| MEA | Lebanon | Beirut |
| PIA | Pakistan | Karachi |
| Saudia | Saudi Arabia | Riyadh |
| TWA | USA | New York |
| Varig | Brazil | São Paulo |
| Viasa | Venezuela | Caracas |
| British Airways | Britain | Heathrow |

## 28.5  As easy as winking: some useful idioms

When would you use these expressions to describe people:

| As | | as a | |
|---|---|---|---|
| | drunk | | lord |
| | sober | | judge |
| | quiet | | mouse |
| | crafty | | fox |
| | white | | sheet |
| | fit | | fiddle |
| | pretty | | picture |
| | quick | | flash |
| | fresh | | daisy |
| | poor | | church mouse |
| | light | | feather |
| | mad | | hatter |
| | proud | | peacock |
| | deaf | | post |
| | sick | | dog |

| As | | as | |
|---|---|---|---|
| | good | | gold |
| | ugly | | sin |
| | thick | | two short planks   ( = stupid) |

## 29.4  'The United Kingdom'

56M
240,000 sq km
7
Birmingham
5–16
July
January
November
635
2,000 km

**30.1    Home cooking: essential language**

| *Utensils and gadgets* | | *Preparation* | |
|---|---|---|---|
| frying pan | plate | peel | teaspoonful |
| saucepan | dish | slice | dessertspoonful |
| casserole | bowl | chop | tablespoonful |
| chopping board | | mince | |
| wooden spoon | | mix | |
| spatula | | stir | |
| ladle | | whip | |
| electric mixer | | whisk | |
| | | beat | |

| *Ingredients* | | | | *Cooking* | |
|---|---|---|---|---|---|
| beef | flour | carrots | apples | boil | raw |
| pork | cornflour | cucumber | pears | fry | (very) rare |
| lamb | salt | courgettes | peaches | roast | medium rare |
| veal | pepper | aubergines | apricots | steam | medium |
| bacon | herbs | celery | raspberries | bake | well-done |
| ham | spices | lettuce | blackcurrants | stew | over-cooked |
| turkey | | onions | plums | grill | |
| duck | | beans | greengages | | |
| chicken | | asparagus | grapefruit | | |

**35.2    In the street . . .**

Gentleman: What's your dog barking at?
Lady: I think he's barking at you.
Gentleman: For God's sake, stop it barking!
Lady: Don't call it 'it', it's a 'he'. It's alright, it's stopped now.
Gentleman: Good! What's its name?
Lady: Although he hasn't got any spots, he's called 'Spot'.
Gentleman: What sort of dog is he?
Lady: He's a Scottish greyhound.
Gentleman: That's not a very well-known breed, is it?
Lady: He's the only one in England, as far as I know.
Gentleman: No wonder he barks at everyone!

**35.3    On the telephone . . .**

A: Hallo?
B: Hallo. Who's that?
A: It's me.
B: Who's *me*?
A: Why me of course.
B: Yes I know it's you, but who are you?
A: I've told you who I am – I'm me.
B: I know you're you, but I still don't know who you are. Anyway, I don't want to talk to you whoever you are – I really want Mrs Jones.
A: Who do you want?
B: Mrs Jones.
A: Mrs Jones? Who's Mrs Jones?
B: Why, Mrs Jones lives where you are, doesn't she?
A: There's no Mrs Jones here. What number do you want?
B: I want Bournemouth 650283.
A: This is Bournemouth 650823.
B: Oh dear, I *am* sorry. I must have dialled the wrong number.
A: It's quite alright.
B: I'll try dialling again. Sorry to have troubled you.
A: It's quite alright. Goodbye.
B: Goodbye.


**35.4    Inverted commas**

'You know, Peter,' said Mary, 'I don't think you've heard a word I've just said, really.'
'I have!'
'Why were you looking out of the window then, Peter?'
'I thought I heard Alan's car arriving – that's all,' said Peter, 'but I was wrong.'
'Well, I'm not going to say it all again.'
'I *did* hear you!' insisted Peter, 'I always listen to what you say … You know I'm sure that's Alan's car this time … Yes it is!'
'Well, are you going to open the door?'
'Certainly not – he's your brother!'
'Alright, *I* will then.'


**37.2    Foreign languages**

a) Albanian
b) Hungarian
c) French
d) Esperanto
e) German
f) Spanish
g) Dutch
h) Portuguese

i) Turkish
j) Polish
k) Italian
l) Finnish
m) Swedish
n) Welsh
o) Latin

## 37.7 Understanding American English

| USA | | GB | USA | | GB |
|---|---|---|---|---|---|
| apartment | = | flat | baggage | = | luggage |
| faucet | = | tap | vacation | = | holidays |
| elevator | = | lift | mailman | = | postman |
| drapes | = | curtains | ZIP code | = | postcode |
| the john | = | the loo (toilet) | mortician | = | undertaker |
| garbage | = | rubbish | bar tender | = | barman |
| closet | = | cupboard | public school | = | state school |
| wash up | = | wash your hands | movie theater | = | cinema |
| cookie | = | biscuit | schedule | = | timetable |
| potato chips | = | crisps | buddy | = | friend |
| candy | = | sweets | swell | | |
| the Fall | = | Autumn | neat | = | nice |
| downtown | = | town centre | cute | | |
| dating | = | going out with | | | |

the letter 'Z' is pronounced 'Zee' in USA, 'Zed' in GB

## 37.8 Understanding non-standard British English

| Scottish | | English | Children | | Adults |
|---|---|---|---|---|---|
| a wee house | = | small house | bunny | = | rabbit |
| a bonny bairn | = | pretty child | moo-cow | = | cow |
| a brae | = | hillside | din-dins | = | dinner |
| a loch | = | lake | bye-byes | = | sleep |
| an advocate | = | lawyer | granny | = | grandmother |
| a kirk | = | church | pussy | = | cat |
| a laddie | = | boy | choo-choo | = | train |
| a lassie | = | girl | piggywig | = | pig |
| aye! | = | Yes! | bikkie | = | biscuit |
| to blether | = | talk nonsense | gee-gee | = | horse |
| a Sassenach | = | Englishman | baa-lamb | = | lamb |
| | | | doggie | = | dog |
| | | | tummy-ache | = | stomach ache |
| | | | wee-wee | = | pee, urinate |
| | | | All gone! | = | I've finished |

## 49.1   A–B

| | |
|---|---|
| He apologized | for |
| I'm not accustomed | to |
| I can't approve | of |
| He was accused | of |
| He was ashamed | of |
| Do you agree | with |
| He seemed annoyed | about |
| We argued all night | about |
| He was astonished | at |
| Are you aware | of |
| What's your attitude | to |
| I'm rather anxious | about |
| What's the advantage | of |
| I believe | in |
| He boasted to us | about |
| You can't blame me | for |
| That car belongs | to |
| I borrowed it | from |

## 49.2   C–D

| | |
|---|---|
| He's capable | of |
| Congratulations | on |
| She's crazy | about |
| Try to concentrate | on |
| The police charged him | with |
| The garage charged him £50 | for |
| They're always complaining | about |
| Give me your comments | on |
| You'll have to choose | between |
| My family consists | of |
| This is characteristic | of |
| I disagree | with |
| I disapprove | of |
| I'm dissatisfied | with |
| He was a bit doubtful | about |
| Cheers! Let's drink | to |
| There's been a delay | in |
| We eventually decided | against |
| I've had a little difficulty | with |

## 49.3  E–H

| | |
|---|---|
| He was very enthusiastic | about |
| I'm feeling excited | about |
| I have a lot of experience | in |
| I feel quite envious | of |
| I'm an expert | on |
| Excuse me | for |
| I don't feel | like |
| How do you feel | about |
| I'm quite fond | of |
| I'm fed up | with |
| Forgive me | for |
| They're famous | for |
| We forgot | about |
| I'm frightened | of |
| She's friendly | with |
| He was found guilty | of |
| That tie doesn't go | with |
| He's always grumbling | about |
| She was gentle | with |
| Have you heard | about |
| There's no hope | of |

## 49.4  I–O

| | |
|---|---|
| I'm very interested | in |
| Please don't interfere | with |
| She insisted | on |
| I'd like some information | about |
| I have no intention | of |
| She's very involved | with |
| Have you heard the joke | about |
| She's always kind | to |
| I know a lot | about |
| It's rude to laugh | at |
| Don't ever lend money | to |
| Our team lost | to |
| He's taken a liking | to |
| My mother looks | like |
| I'm going on holiday – can you look | after |
| Last year he got married | to |
| Where are you going?   Are you making | for |
| What's the matter | with |
| Their son was named | after |
| Take no notice | of |
| Have you heard any news | of |
| What's your opinion | about |
| I object | to |

**49.5   P–Q**

| | |
|---|---|
| I'm very pleased | with |
| I was presented | with |
| I'm a bit puzzled | about |
| He's very proud | of |
| How much did you pay | for |
| They provided him | with |
| He protested | about |
| I couldn't ever part | with |
| They prevented him | from |
| He was punished | for |
| It's time to prepare | for |
| I'm pessimistic | about |
| He's very popular | with |
| He needs protection | from |
| I'm well qualified | for |

**49.6   R–S**

| | |
|---|---|
| He's much respected | for |
| What is the result | of |
| Who's responsible | for |
| I've read a report | on |
| What's your reaction | to |
| 'Moon' rhymes | with |
| You can't rely | on |
| There's no room here | for |
| Try to get rid | of |
| Are you related | to |
| Nobody's safe | from |
| She's in bed suffering | from |
| I can't work out the solution | to |
| I'm suspicious | of |
| He succeeded | in |
| If he's angry, just smile | at |
| I feel sorry | for |
| I've made a study | of |
| Are you serious | about |
| She was sympathetic | with |
| I'm sick | of |
| They saved him | from |
| AA stands | for |

## 49.7 T–Z

| | |
|---|---|
| He's just like his father – he takes | after |
| He was talked | out of |
| He was talked | into |
| Stop talking | about |
| I'm tired | of |
| There should be a tax | on |
| What's the trouble | with |
| I've been thinking | of |
| What's the use | of |
| I can't get used | to |
| There are thousands of victims | of |
| I've already warned you | about |
| Don't worry | about |
| What's wrong | with |
| She has a great zest | for |

## 50.1 A–B

| | |
|---|---|
| in | agreement. |
| by | accident. |
| in | advance. |
| with | an accent. |
| for | ages. |
| under | age. |
| on | the agenda. |
| with | open arms. |
| out of | the blue. |
| in | the same boat. |
| on | the brain. |
| without | a break. |
| on | business. |
| on | his behalf. |
| under | my breath. |
| out of | breath. |

## 50.2 C–D

| | |
|---|---|
| by | chance. |
| for | a change. |
| off | your chest. |
| in | the clouds. |
| off | colour. |
| in | common. |
| in | confidence. |
| under | control. |
| at | all costs. |
| in | command. |
| in | charge. |
| on | a diet. |
| in | the dark. |
| up to | date. |
| out of | my depth. |
| under | discussion. |
| on | duty. |

## 50.3 E–G

| | |
|---|---|
| on | edge. |
| at | a loose end. |
| at | the end. |
| in | the end. |
| in | favour. |
| without | fail. |
| on | fire. |
| in | flames. |
| in | flower. |
| out of | focus. |
| on | foot. |
| on | form. |
| at | a glance. |
| for | good. |
| at | a guess. |

## 50.5 L–M

| | |
|---|---|
| at | last. |
| at | large. |
| at | the latest. |
| at | least. |
| at | great length. |
| in | length. |
| in | my light. |
| between | the lines. |
| on | loan. |
| at | a loss. |
| for | love. |
| out of | luck. |
| by | marriage. |
| by | all means. |
| on | my mind. |
| in | two minds. |
| by | mistake. |
| in | mourning. |
| in | the mood. |

## 50.4 H–K

| | |
|---|---|
| by | heart. |
| in | hand. |
| off | hand. |
| in | good hands. |
| off | his head. |
| in | height. |
| for | hire. |
| on | holiday. |
| on | the hour. |
| in | the small hours. |
| on | the house. |
| in | his honour. |
| in | your own interest. |
| with | interest. |
| on | the increase. |
| out of | a job. |
| to | my knowledge. |

## 50.6 N–P

| | |
|---|---|
| by | name. |
| in | the news. |
| for | nothing. |
| in | the nude. |
| for | once. |
| by | one. |
| on | order. |
| in | order. |
| out of | order. |
| in | pain. |
| in | person. |
| out of | place. |
| in | practice. |
| out of | print. |
| on | principle. |
| in | principle. |

## 50.7   Q-R

| | |
|---|---|
| out of | the question. |
| on | the radio. |
| at | random. |
| for | ransom. |
| under | repair. |
| by | request. |
| in | reserve. |
| in | some respects. |
| in | return. |
| in | revenge. |
| in | the right. |
| on | the rocks. |
| as | a rule. |
| in | the long run. |
| in | a rut. |

## 50.8   S

| | |
|---|---|
| in | safety. |
| for | my sake. |
| behind | schedule. |
| from | scratch. |
| in | season. |
| on | second thoughts. |
| in | self-defence. |
| in | his shoes. |
| for | short. |
| on | show. |
| by | sight. |
| out of | sight. |
| on | spec. |
| on | the spot. |
| at | stake. |
| in | stock. |
| in | store. |
| on | strike. |
| without | success. |
| above | suspicion. |
| in | full swing. |

## 50.9   T

| | |
|---|---|
| on | tape. |
| in | bad taste. |
| on | television. |
| on | good terms. |
| in | theory. |
| at | a time. |
| before | my time. |
| from | time to time. |
| in | time. |
| in | good time. |
| in | no time at all. |
| on | time. |
| behind | the times. |
| on | trial. |
| in | tune. |
| in | touch. |

## 50.10   U-W

| | |
|---|---|
| in | uniform. |
| of | no use. |
| in | use. |
| in | vain. |
| of | great value. |
| in | verse. |
| on | view? |
| on | a visit. |
| at | war. |
| without | warning. |
| in | a way. |
| in | the way. |
| under | way. |
| under | the weather. |
| in | weight. |
| for | a while. |
| in | width. |
| for | word. |
| in | writing. |